AF492415

MY SONG

MOVING FROM CHILDHOOD ABUSE TO GRATITUDE

DOROTHEA JUNO-JOHNSTON

To my daughters.

FORWARD

I wrote this story with the intention that it would help others coming from beginnings that seem impossible to heal at first glance. Circumstances created the time and space to complete the memoir. Not one to argue with or tempt fate, I sat down to write. And, here we are.

My Dad filled all the criteria for being considered a devout Catholic, by the community we lived in... This devotion included walking the two miles to attend Catholic Mass every day during Lent and Advent. He also insisted the family gather, kneel, and say the rosary together each evening at 7pm. And, of, course, Catholic Grace before dinner was never missed. None of us ever considered that the priests who led our church were not guiding our Dad as God directed, and indeed backed him up all the way as head of our household.

MY SONG: Moving from Childhood Abuse

to Gratitude, tells the story of a spiritual journey. A crazy up and down, slightly deranged journey of my life until my mid-70s. It is one I chose to take, and in some instances, one circumstances brought me to. I think we always have a choice of how to navigate our life journey and what to make of it. The short story told here is a transformation from a child of abuse to a woman healer. The longer story describes the steps, decisions and people along the way who made the whole thing possible. My chosen fields of study in psychology, energy medicine and spiritual emergence inform the perspectives on my journey.

I encourage you to enjoy the ride. Prepare to laugh, cry and release any other emotion that bubble up from these pages. At the outset, I want to state the obvious: this is my personal memoir, my memories of my experiences.

It is nothing short of a miracle, that, having lived my childhood, I matured to be the woman I am today. What follows is the story of my young life, the things that happened that I once thought were unbearable, and some of the people who helped me to survive.

Take what you will, leave what you must. I send wishes for something in these pages to speak to you.

Blessings,

Dorothea

CONTENTS

Chapter One: In the Beginning
Chapter Two: My Father's Death
Chapter Three: Teen Years
Chapter Four: It's Ringing in the Kitchen
or; Who's Really Nuts
Here Anyway
Chapter Five: Waking Up
Chapter Six: Death with Dignity
Chapter Seven: Moving from Surviving to
Thriving
Chapter Nine: Therapeutic Touch (TT)
Chapter Ten: Mystical and Magical
Times
Chapter Eleven: Spiritual Awakening
Chapter Twelve: And the Beat Goes On...

Afterward
Appendix: Songs
Notes & Suggested Readings

CHAPTER ONE

IN THE BEGINNING

In the dream, it is a hot summer night. I am almost four years old, sitting on the floor by the front bedroom window, which was low to the ground, and I can just see out and get some air, hoping that Daddy will not see me.

Daddy is coming up the stairs and there is no place to hide. Please someone help me... I hear the sound of his footsteps across the bedroom floor. They sound black, forceful, one step slightly lighter than the other. One foot hit the floor slightly harder, reminiscent of his limp. Sitting there on the floor near the window, fear rises in my throat. I don't know what is coming. I am watching for him, afraid to breathe

I am the youngest of twelve children, born in 1940 in a small town outside Boston, Massachusetts. We were Brady, Martha, Janet, Lydia, Stephen, and Betsy who died eight years before my birth, Bethany, Eileen, Jean, Sue, and Gordon. The family, including my parents, numbered thirteen. Our country was poised to enter World War II, and Brady left for basic training a year after my birth. The 1950s comedy movie, Cheaper by the Dozen, does not come close to my experience of living in a big family, and I saw nothing funny about it when I saw it years ago. It could be very hard for the parents and the children to live in a family that large.

We were a Catholic family of Irish and Scottish ancestry. Dad worked as a meat inspector for the United States Government. My mother Victoria was a stoic Scots woman who learned to raise her children by nurturing them with food and good humor. She was not a demonstrative emotional person; not often would you hear her say "I love you," but somehow you knew she did.

My parents were from an era when, at least in their culture, it was expected that couples would have as many children as God sent them. It was their way of life. The Dad, especially a Devout Catholic, as neighbors and friends referred to mine, was head of the household. No one dared to question what he did or didn't do. His wife deferred to him always. Strict discipline in the form of brutal physical, psychological and sexual abuse by my father was part of my daily life.

We were often reminded, through the teachings of the church, that we were bad, sinful. If we thought of ourselves as good, that, in *itself* condemned us. Our family said the Rosary every night. On the nights that I knelt beside my brother Gordon we got the giggles. I was sent to bed early for this, my brother was not. I often felt singled out by Daddy when more than one person was involved in inexcusable behavior. Now I see it was a way to send me upstairs, away from the rest of the family. To the family this seemed harsh maybe, but not sinister.

It was at night, upstairs, that the punishment came. It was frightening, hard to understand and unpredictable. I would be lying on the floor desperately pushing the blanket off of my face. His large hands held the blanket round my neck while doing things I wouldn't yet understand to my body. I learned to hold my breath and he would let go just as I thought I would die. I would lie perfectly still on the floor; just this side of death. No words were spoken: he would get up and go away from me.

As I got a little older the punishment changed. I could feel his heavy body on me. Again, I thought I would die of the pain in my body from his pushing inside. Maybe my legs would break. If I cried, he would say; "Stop that crying or I'll give you something to cry about!" I choked; I stopped crying. No more words were spoken.

When my father was at home, I wasn't allowed to speak unless an adult asked me a question. Still, there is a spark in me that knew to just speak up at times—despite and damn the consequences. I often received an unwarranted smack on the head for my trouble, but that spark would not be held down. My siblings did not take notice of these things lest his attention be drawn to them. I learned from three of my sisters, much later in life, when I first began to recall these memories and to talk to them, that they also had been raped by Dad. One of my sisters said it didn't stop until she was fourteen and she finally fought him off. The wall of silence prevailed.

Some of my sisters paid special attention to me even in the craziness of such a large family. Bethany did her best to protect me from Dad. When I was crying, she would come up to see if she could help, but if Dad caught her doing this, he yelled to leave the crybaby alone. I did not know if my sisters and brothers were scared. I don't think it ever occurred to me back then to think about that. It turned out later that some of them were, and they got good at living the lie as I did most of the time; some of them did help me when they could.

After my third or fourth year, I used to cry a little any time I felt afraid. My sisters and brothers called me crybaby. I'm sure they could not think about what the cry baby stuff was all about. "You and Gordon were always so spoiled," Lydia used to say. She even called me a spoiled brat. I wonder now, how did she know I was spoiled? But, certainly not in the way she meant. I was rarely without fear or dread.

On some nights, when Daddy came, all I saw were black swirling circles much like a black ant hill. I could barely breathe, when I opened my eyes, there were the black circles.

In the morning I would go downstairs and complain, "Mommy, my throat hurts."

"Come here darling; let me see how you are."

She would hold my forehead with her other hand on the back of my head. "It doesn't feel like you have a fever, maybe some warm salt water will help." Then she would fix the warm salt water and teach me how to gargle with it.

Mom's presence was comforting, though it changed nothing with Dad. She enjoyed watching us girls brush and comb each others hair—another very proper way to take care of each other physically. Mom seemed to encourage these kinds of things. She also enjoyed just being around us as we chatted, giggled or whatever we did while fixing each other up.

Mom took charge of many difficult situations and did what had to be done without complaint or tears. One of the gifts she passed on to me was the ability to cope in a crisis. As one of the family, I saw her cry only three times in my entire life. She had a habit of sitting at the table talking to herself in a whisper. I wondered what fears and disappointments she had beneath her stoic exterior. She often said she did not want any of her daughters to have twelve children.

Her sense of humor sustained her, I suspect, as mine has sustained me. It is the underlying gift she gave to each of us – a sense of timing. We laughed a lot. She put up with loud music for years and loved it when her family sang while doing household chores.

Every afternoon, about the time her children arrived home from school, Mom would be taking bread out of the oven. "Put your books away, wash your hands and come out to table – rolls are ready." This was her way to let us know she loved us, of that I am sure.

I have no memories of being held in a loving way as a very small child. Still, Mom showed me love as best she knew how. It seems to me she took advantage when one of us was sick or not feeling well, to touch us as part of taking care of the illness.

While we children had our afternoon snack, she'd be peeling potatoes and breaking green beans to go with the roast for supper. Sometimes we got to help with beans and other parts of the meal. Mom learned to cook for her father and brothers growing up on the family farm at Hey Cove, Nova Scotia and it was how she took care of all of us.

Being nurtured by my sister Janet stands out for me. Janet was my godmother. Years later I came to understand that her gift to me was unconditional love. One day, at about the age of five, Janet dressed me up all in white to take me to the Franklin Park Zoo. After I was ready to go, her instructions were to "stay close by while I get dressed." My five-year-old mind interpreted staying close as anywhere in the house. This particular day I chose to wait in the coal bin in our basement which was what I considered my "safe place" in our home. When Janet called to me to say she was ready to go, I came up from the basement. It never occurred to me that I was covered in coal dust until she said. "Dorothea, how did you get so dirty so fast? Come on, we'll have to get you cleaned up."

I was a child who was used to being severely punished by my father for the tiniest infraction or for no reason at all that I understood. If he had been there to see how "bad" I had been, the day would have been painful and scary. Even though I learned later Janet "could have killed me," she never let on to me how upset she was at the time. We went about the business of getting me cleaned up and ready to go again. This included Janet taking off the dress, washing, drying and ironing it (I never have figured out how she managed to do that in 1945), and cleaning me up to wear it. This time she did not let me out of her sight till we were ready to go. What I do know is we still got to go to the Zoo. Janet, her then boyfriend Craig, and I had such a good time. Craig, over time, showed me how a loving father behaved and treated me with kindness always.

Surely the words were not with me as a child, but inside something helped me to know you could be loved even when you were "bad." Janet was my fairy godmother as well as my spiritual godmother. There were many others who helped in similar ways. They gave me hope to believe there was a way out of the struggle and they loved me in their own way. My life would have been very different on so many levels without all these folks in my formative years to guide me.

During those malleable years, music played a large part of daily existence in our family. Singing was something my father seemed to like. I enjoy memories of performing for aunts and uncles on Sundays when they came to visit. It was one of a very few times when I was encouraged to be heard. My siblings and I often sang while we were doing the dishes after big family meals or cleaning the house together on

Saturdays. Singing made us all feel happy to be together and gave us a sense of security. These moments gave me relief from the scary times.

Some dreams came as nightmares. I believe it was a way for my unconscious to let go of the demons in the night. It was the way I was beginning to dream. No specific dream comes to mind, just this vague remembrance of being terrified as a young child. Many children have the usual "bad guys" in the closet, but mine took on a whole new life in the years of wondering when he would come.

My father had a very specific way to keep me from trusting my memories or my experience. Sometimes he would ask me a question, such as, "Did you make all the markings on this wall?" My brother Gordon and I had scribbled on it and we had to wash the markings off. "I did some of them," I answered.

"Stick out your tongue," I tremble as I stuck it out; I was about seven years old.

"Your tongue is black," he'd say, "you're lying." I knew I was not lying. He created doubt and fear, confusion. Never trusting what I knew to be true created a sense of not knowing *anything*, and helped to foster the mental illness that would plague me for years.

It never occurred to me that *he* was lying. This scene was repeated often, so even if I was remembering the things that happened at night, I would have doubted them. Dad's method of creating doubt for me was instilled at an early age.

Sometimes I loved him and tried very hard to get his attention. I loved him, or, at the very least I wanted him to love me. You'd see me running up the street to meet him on his way home from the Boston market after a day of shopping for food. Running just to see if I could carry a bundle home and help him. My hope was that he would smile at me, or talk kindly to me, or hold my hand - any kindness would have been okay. I don't know exactly what I was looking for, but I was looking while the rest was blocked out of my mind. I even repressed the accusations about my black tongue though they were all still going on. "Please, I was saying with my actions, please Daddy, just love me." Later, much later, I suspected that he must have been afraid of me. Afraid I would talk and tell what happened. How could he know that I had already buried it, and the rest of the family saw only what they could tolerate?

Many nights I got severe leg aches that prohibited me from going to sleep. Lydia or Bethany would come up to my bedroom, especially after I turned eight or nine, to rub my legs for me to see if that could help me sleep. I wonder if my legs ached because I wanted to run away from it all, but couldn't. There is also the possibility I got the leg aches so that someone would touch me. It's not the same as being held, but it felt good and it was a way of getting some physical touching that was healing not painful. I remember lying there feeling the ache, but loving the warm hands rubbing up and down so I could sleep. Both Lydia and Bethany had to do this quietly so Daddy would not know they were "coddling" me. They were very quiet about it, but did it many times. It was very loving and safe touch.

While all the ravages at home were going on, there were other people who helped create miracles for me. My Uncle Kevin gave me room to speak at his house and loved me just as I was.

Uncle Kevin is playing with a jig saw puzzle. The pieces may be too small for him to put together. Make sure the baby doesn't see him with it or she will want it. Babies are like that. She has a puzzle of her own with bigger pieces but she'll want the one you have if she sees it. Actually, there are several puzzles near her with mostly big pieces, but they are all getting mixed up together.

This dream tells me that Uncle Kevin knew there were things he could help with even if he didn't have all the pieces of the puzzle. The baby is clearly my young self not understanding so many things that went on in my life. While in graduate school, I wrote the following poem for Uncle Kevin.

Rare Old Irish Coins

He rolled me up and down the porch on a
Table with wheels
He listened to me talk.
He let me punch the air in imitation
Of him imitating the boxers
He spoke to me of personal things.
He let me know that he knew there was pain
He heard what I could not say.
These things he gave to me
Over my lifetime
He was my father's brother and he saved my life

It strikes me as strange that no one ever talked about sex or the sexual act in our house, even though there was so much abuse going on. There was a conspiracy of silence – I mean, you can't talk about it, can you? I am aware that some of my siblings didn't see my father's harsh side at all. In early 1952, Jo Stafford had a popular hit record "As You Desire Me," which my sister Lydia bought home. I remember when she played it, my father became so enraged that he broke the record in half and demanded no such thing every be played in our house. Lydia was so repentant and stated that Daddy would never have gotten so angry if there wasn't a good reason. She was contrite and so sorry. Daddy was the best in the world from Lydia's perspective. I was a few months shy of my twelfth birthday, standing on the sidelines watching this.

Derrick Jensen so aptly put it in his book "A Language Older Than Words"; "the worst thing my father did was the denial *that any of it ever occurred.*" Describing his own childhood, he writes, "We became a family of amnesiacs. There's no place in the mind to sufficiently contain these experiences. The willingness to forget is the essence of silencing."

Judith Herman writes in "Trauma and Recovery"; "Certain violations of the social compact are too terrible to utter aloud: this is the meaning of the word *unspeakable*."

I think now, the level of denial in our family was irreversible and what memories we did have, came infrequently. I, like everyone else, had the family amnesia. In our family, the way to survive was that no one in the family remembered the horrendous things that actually happened. It was all so crazy: nothing was crazier than being in that house.

CHAPTER TWO

MY FATHER'S DEATH

It is August 1952, very late at night. I am 12, Dad is in the hospital; I hear Mom come home and I walk down the stairs from one of the two large bedrooms that I share with all my sisters. Most of my siblings and mother are gathered in the living room standing around and crying. Mom puts her arms around me to hold me. I know my father has just died but cannot say anything.

"Mom, you need to tell her," I hear my sisters say. "She knows something is wrong." In these few moments my mind is blank and I have no memory of just what Mom did say to me that night. I am afraid to tell them I know Daddy is dead for fear they will know that I wished for this and that it is my fault. I am so afraid of my father and his abuse that I wished for his death many times. In fact, fear is the only emotion I feel at this moment.

The next few days pass in a bit of a blur for me. On the day of the wake I overhear the discussion between my Mom and siblings about whether or not they should send me to stay with one of the neighbors while the rest of the family goes to the funeral parlor for the wake. I protest rather loudly. I am frightened to be sent away from the family and excluded from the wake, even though I don't really know what that is. They decide I will go with the family. A navy dress appropriate for a twelve-year-old is bought.

We all pile into cars and go to the funeral home. No one tells me that I will see my father there and I feel shocked to see him in his coffin. He looks very real to me. Fear crawls up my throat. I am on verge of choking. I hear my sister Janet crying and saying to one of my brothers, "He looked so real I thought he was going to sit up and talk to me!" Her words helped me believe he could get up out of the coffin and come after me. I can barely breathe, but manage to find a corner to hide in for a while.

The funeral Mass is the next morning. I am wearing the white dress of my Confirmation. Nausea is my constant companion and it is not possible for me to ride in the limousine to church. My Dad's sister offers to walk to church so I won't have to get in the car. In the church it is dark, scary, and my fear level rises. A caring cousin takes me by the hand outside for some comforting and ginger ale. I do not know what to say to her. "It's okay to be sad," she says. I don't feel sad, only afraid. Questions run through my head. Will they find out that this is my entire fault? What will happen to me?

I am told I went to the cemetery for the burial but have no memory of that part of the day. Back home my sisters tell everyone to change clothes and put on bright dresses, as if somehow wearing bright clothes will make it all better, cheer Mom up so she is not so sad. I look at Mom who does not look as if seeing bright colors will make her feel better.

Later, I climb back up the stairs to my bedroom and curl into a ball to keep myself safe. It is new to feel safe in my bed. Is it true he is really gone? So far no one has accused me of anything; maybe they don't know and won't know that I wanted him to die.

My father's death helped me to begin to feel safe in my home. His death was a new beginning for me. I was able to breathe. I was allowed to speak. Breathing allows one to move in life. It does not, however erase all the years of terror.

CHAPTER THREE

TEEN YEARS

Mostly, my teen years were better off not remembered. I was shy, backward with boys and had one of the world's worst cases of acne by the age of fourteen. From my perspective, the acne on my face offered itself up as the reason for my unhappiness. By that time, all traces of my early struggles with my Dad were gone from my conscious memory. I blamed the acne for giving me the feeling of being too ugly to have a boyfriend. I never dated throughout junior high or high school. I had some contact with boys through my friends who had boyfriends, but no dating for me. I was a very good, sometimes even gifted, student, which helped me get along.

A group of girlfriends formed around me in grammar school and stayed with me through high school. They gave me connections outside my family. I was, and continue to be, enormously grateful for my girlfriends through my school years and my women friends through my entire life. Mom loved and was very welcoming to all of our friends over the years. They loved to hang out at our house. We managed to laugh a fair amount, go to school football and hockey games and have fun at pajama parties. No one seemed to notice my abject misery. I had this underlying feeling that I was just no good. It saddened me so much that I had to pretend a lot, even with girlfriends. I was a follower and would do most anything my close friends suggested.

In eighth grade, like a robot responding to programming, I went through my confirmation as a Catholic. I wonder if I had any idea what it meant to be confirmed. I remained a Catholic for many years, going through the obligatory Masses by rote, even going to confession, which was terrifying, because I couldn't think of what my sins were. Like so many others, I made some up so the priest wouldn't think I was too righteous for my own good. (If I had had less fear and more humor about it, maybe I would have made up some really good ones. Alas, that was not to be.)

Every year, Aunt Bethany would invite me for a week at a time to her house and shower me with attention and love, all the while making sure I knelt beside my bed to say my prayers at night. That's how I learned that prayer was not followed by pain. These visits started when I was young and continued right up until the time I left home to marry.

For my family, music was the glue that held all of us together. We sang cleaning house, doing dishes and any other time we felt like it. With music of course, came dancing. At least it did in our family. Stephen used to pick me up and dance me around before I could walk. He encouraged me to keep dancing as a teenager. There was always a record player with the latest Pop music playing – quite loudly I might add. No wonder Mom went deaf, after so many years of loud teen music.

During my late teens and early twenties, when I came in out of a very cold day, Mom would greet me with, "Come here, Dottie, put your hands under my arms and let me warm them for you." This warming of my hands was a way for her to hug me at the same time. It felt so comforting each time she offered this caring. Mom was continuing to find ways to love us without showing too much outward emotion. It was during this time that Mom and I first shared humor with each other. It was Mom, siblings who looked out for one another, and many caring people, singing and dancing that helped me rise up out of the pain in that house.

In high school my junior English teacher befriended me and let me know that, at least to her, I was special. I am grateful to her for seeing what I could not say. She and my guidance counselor did everything they could to talk me into going to college. All I knew was that I had to get a job right away to help support my mother. Dad's work had provided Social Security payments for Mom and us children until we were eighteen. Mom's job continued to be taking care of us and our home. I know my older siblings contributed to the family financially for many years. However, by the time I reached high school, most had married and left home. I went to work at the local bank directly after high school.

I met Bruce the man I'd later marry, at a church young adult group. We did many group activities together. There was bowling club on Sunday nights, ski trips to New Hampshire once a year and lots of parties with hired bands for dancing. We had much fun and I, for a time, seemed to pull up out of my earlier sadness.

Nightmares about demons that had loud

intruding voices in the night came right after I started dating Bruce. By the time I was 20, I would wake up nearly nightly screaming that there were snakes in my bed. Mom could hear me from downstairs. Scared, she'd call to Gordon in the next room to go in and wake me up. "You have to wake her up, Gordon; she could die in her sleep from fright. Make sure she gets all the way out of bed and is really awake."

I am asleep in my bed at home. I realize there are snakes crawling through my legs; I am trying to get them off and screaming at the same time. No matter what I do, they will not leave me be.

Bless Gordon. He often got me up, pulled all the covers off my bed to show me there were no snakes. The snake dreams came often at that time of my life. I was only beginning to think of Bruce in a sexual way. No doubt it was frightening to my unconscious. I suspect that any sexual feelings at all were terrifying to me.

If I had to give a reason why I married Bruce,

I would be hard pressed to think of one. At one point I broke off the relationship, not knowing why for sure. Mom called Bruce and told him I was miserable; I don't think I was. I believe I was confused about what would come next for the two of us. Bruce called again to see me and we picked up, in a way, where we had left off. I did what was expected of women my age at that time. I married for what I thought then was love and for children. We met when I was nineteen and married in September of 1962 when I was twenty-two. Just like so many others of our generation, we were on our way to living happily ever after.

MY SONG

CHAPTER FOUR

IT'S RINGING IN THE KITCHEN OR; WHO'S REALLY NUTS HERE ANYWAY?

It was a dream wedding, the kind those of us growing up in the 1950s thought we should have. All of my sisters and brothers, plus Bruce's cousins were attendants. My mother was so proud. Her baby was getting married! I was caught up in being the center of wonderful attention for the first time in my life. It was a lovely, fun wedding for all.

What I knew about being married, however, was very little. I had total amnesia about my years of abuse, and never having had a conversation with my Mom about sexuality I had no understanding of my body. I felt confused and scared, and Bruce was little more prepared than I was. In the first year of our marriage, I began to exhibit signs of mental illness. I saw black curly spots on the wall moving in circles sometimes when I was frightened. Or, more likely, seeing the black curly spots is what frightened me and made me question what was wrong with me. I imagined things were crawling on my arms and there are pictures of me taken in that first year of marriage showing me wearing long sleeves to cover my scratching. Our family doctor suggested it might be better if I lived away from my large, loving, but overpowering family. Moving away from Boston seemed to be the answer. We moved first to Phoenix, Arizona in 1963. We chose Phoenix because my sister Lydia was raising her family there, so I would know at least one person.

Moving away did not forestall the overt

appearance of depression in the years to come. Major changes don't come easily for me and torrential, gut wrenching tears accompanied that move, which would be the first of many. I remember getting my new state license picture taken when the news of the assassination of President Kennedy came on the television in the Motor Vehicle Department. I, shocked and unbelieving at this news, burst into tears. The man took my picture and I lived with that picture on my license for the next four years. The country was reeling, but the assassination gave me an acceptable explanation for all the crying I was doing. I was pregnant and Mom came out to Phoenix to help me with my first pregnancy. Elizabeth, our first child, came into our family in August, 1964. We were overjoyed and more than a little awed by her.

Bruce got a job in 1966 with the Federal Credit Union Administration, and Cleveland, Ohio was our next move. Cleveland brought us close enough to drive to Boston for the holidays. Being able to drive to Boston seemed to soften the blow of leaving my sister Lydia and her family. We lived in Cleveland for nine months; I've always said that it was the longest three years of my life. It is the only place I have ever lived where I could not make friends. I suspect this was partly because I was newly pregnant, not feeling well, and the few neighborhood people I met made it clear they were not interested I making new friends.

When news came that we were to transfer to Chicago, I was happy to do so. Our second daughter, Jane, joined us in September 1967 after we had moved to Park Forest, Illinois, about forty miles south of Chicago. During the Illinois years, my depression seemed to be sneaking up on me. My state of health while pregnant was attributed to morning sickness and no one seemed to understand that the symptoms I was experiencing were much more than that. Depression and fear are not always visible. I kept busy.

It was in Park Forest that I first picked up a guitar. Teaching myself how to play, along with help from a neighbor and some beginner guitar books, gave structure to the music that was already an important part of my life. I was determined to learn to play. Every day I practiced when the girls were napping. It was exciting to be able to play along with songs I had been singing most of my life. Pete Seeger's "Where have all the Flowers gone" was the first complete song I learned. I was amazed how many songs I could play with only a few chords.

The whole neighborhood would sit in the back yard on a summer evening. It was a great atmosphere for me and other beginning guitar players. One of our neighbors called out the chord changes ahead of time for those of us learning to play and we all sang along. It was a lively and happy time. Or, so it seemed on the outside. Inside, I was beginning to feel the effects of the depression which was now my daily companion. I ate more food than I needed to see if that would keep the fear at bay. I had the sense that something was not right with me, but I had no idea what that something was.

My third pregnancy came when my depression could be described as severe. I did not know how to cope. More food was my answer to my increasing and inalterable fear. The pregnancy did not bring on the depression. They were present at the same time. By then I was shaking on the outside as well as inside. On a home visit to Boston, my sister Martha confessed to me that she had been diagnosed with schizophrenia and urged me to find a psychiatrist as well.

I found and began seeing a psychiatrist in downtown Chicago. He did his best to help me. Near the end of that pregnancy, the word came down that we were being transferred to Cincinnati, Ohio. My reaction: "Cincinnati, Ohio, who the hell ever heard of Cincinnati, Ohio?" The thought of moving to another new place frightened me, given my emotional state. Our youngest daughter Emma was born in July, 1970. A few months later we left our friends in Park Forest and moved to Cincinnati. Once again, our country was in turmoil. Students protesting the Vietnam War at Kent State were gunned down on May 4, 1970, my birthday, just two months before Emma's birth. I was totally unaware of this happening at that time. Focusing on my new baby and growing family was all that I could handle.

Bruce's job in Cincinnati required that he do a lot of traveling. I was thirty years old, feeling totally overwhelmed, and left to my own devices with Emma, Jane, and Elizabeth. This situation worsened my fear, trembling and sense of despair. At the time, I did not recognize that what was happening to me was a developing mental illness. It is only in retrospect that I see this clearly.

In November, 1970, shortly after moving to Cincinnati and on the advice of my psychiatrist, I checked myself into Cauldhill Barnett, a small psychiatric hospital convenient to where we were living. My primary care physician recommended a psychiatrist whom I had seen twice prior to going to the hospital. One day I called him in a panic; he asked if I could get someone to watch the children so I could go to the hospital. My new neighbor agreed to care for the children. It was to be the first of several admissions over a two-year period.

My first admission lasted three months. For the next year or more, I had several admissions; some lasted two weeks and some a month at a time. For the first three months, Elizabeth and Jane went to live with a wonderful group of Catholic sisters we had known back in Park Forest and Emma stayed with her godparents, also in Park Forest. These folks graciously offered to care for the girls and we accepted. We were so new to Cincinnati; our resources there for this kind of help were non-existent.

During my first year as a patient at Cauldhill Barnett, I barely functioned. My psychiatrist protected me from following the arbitrary rules of the institution. It was required that all patients eat their meals in the dining room, but I was not forced to do so. My doctor was categorical in his instruction to the staff on my behalf. "Under no circumstances is she to be required to do anything that she does not want to do," he told them. I was extremely fragile during the early days of that first admission. My depression was so severe I could hardly walk, could not carry on conversations, and was terrified of everyone and everything. Like a person in a trance, I used to walk the hall, totally silent and without awareness of who or where I was. It never occurred to me that I was in a locked ward and could not leave if I wanted to.

Psych Ward

There she was traveling east and

Talking madly to anyone

Who wasn't listening

And there I was traveling west

Silent – afraid to speak to anyone

Who wasn't listening

Each in our own

world…apart…together

Who was to say when our paths

Finally crossed and she

Stopped her running and I

Stopped my shuffling that the laughs
We shared were because
All the time we were
On the same road
At the same time
Doing the same things…apart…together
With everyone who wasn't listening
And who's to say what's madness.

After several weeks I began to talk to a little. A fellow patient was able to coax me to the dining room with the reassurance she would be with me each step of the way. The process of becoming well enough to function in the outside world was long and difficult. Treatment included daily sessions with my psychiatrist and, after a time, weekly group therapy sessions. The group therapy sessions were immensely helpful to my recovery. It was in that group that I first began to speak up for myself and get the courage to talk about what I was feeling. We had a gifted facilitator and the other group members encouraged and helped me.

When I could function to some degree on my own, I was moved to a smaller building (the Annex) across from the main hospital. There was a small room on the first floor of the Annex where patient medications were kept and the telephone was placed when it wasn't in use. Whenever the nurse on duty left her post, she locked the phone in the kitchen. Calls were usually from the main hospital building, in regard to some patient matter. In the past, the patients had been able to take messages and let the nurse know who to call when she returned, but this was no longer allowed. We wondered what fear prompted this decision. Now, the phone would just go on ringing in the kitchen. When the nurse on duty returned to her desk, she did not know who, in the other building, needed to speak with her. We could tell her only that the phone had been ringing. In a sense, we patients took care of ourselves. Our ability to laugh at ourselves, the music we played together and the experience we shared allowed me to become well enough to take care of my family.

During the two-year period that I was in and out of the hospital, Sister Alice came into my life. Our introduction took place while I was functioning at home and not currently in the psychiatric hospital. She was the guidance counselor and music teacher in the local Catholic school my children attended. I reached out to ask for her assurance that the school was a good one for my children. When I told Sister Alice why I had come, she held her hand out to me and said, "So very glad to meet you." It was rare for a parent to come to the school prior to registering her children. She later told me that she saw me as a mother wanting to protect her children. We soon became friends. It seemed destined somehow and I am hugely grateful for the love and caring I and my family have received over the years from Alice.

During the time I spent in the psychiatric hospital, I found Debbie, a friend to play guitar with. She and I forged a bond over the songs we played together. Music helped us back to sanity and gave us diversion from the therapy groups that tended toward the serious nature of our purpose there. I cherished the music we played together and know it was so important to the healing process. We continued our friendship after we both left the hospital and my daughters loved Debbie. I found it difficult to play some of our songs for a long while after her early death, which came about two years after our hospital stay. Debbie was hit by a car while riding a bicycle.

In late October, 1971, I began the last of my hospital admissions. I called Sister Alice from the hospital phone to ask if she could help me find someone to take care of the children. "Bruce is just not able to do this – not able to even ask for help," I told her. Sister Alice found people in our parish who willingly and lovingly took care of our girls. It was a blessing to all of us and allowed Bruce to be with the three of them on weekends.

On a few occasions, Bruce brought the girls to see me. Emma was just a little over a year and climbed all over the bed; Jane was four and mostly wanted me to hold her. Elizabeth, at the age of seven, was old enough to see that things with Mommy were not okay. I suspect it was very hard for her to see all this even though I did my best to pull it together while they were there visiting.

I learned early on that even if you were smart enough to check yourself in and cognizant enough to know you needed help, some of the individuals charged with your well-being stopped listening to anything you said the minute you signed your name on the admission papers. The following story is an example of no one listening.

Four weeks into my last stay there, I was in crisis. I could barely move. I was certain something was physically wrong with my body. Each day, to no avail, I asked my psychiatrist for a medical doctor. One day he sent an egotistical PhD sort in to see me. He asked, "Is there anything I can do for you in your psychiatrist's absence?"

"Yes," I replied, "you can convince him to get me to a medical doctor – there is something physically wrong with me." The symptoms I had, along with an inability to move, included nausea, loss of weight, a nonexistent appetite and extreme fatigue. He told me, "There is nothing wrong with you that making a decision whether or not to go home and take care of your children won't fix. It is indecision that is making you so depressed." Devastated, I left that meeting having fallen deeper into an abyss. Sitting mute and motionless in group therapy that afternoon was all I could manage. The doctor's missile hit its mark, but the target was already down.

My psychiatrist then suggested that he could get me a couple of nights sleep to see if, rested, I still felt the need for a doctor. He ordered Thorazine for me, a drug usually prescribed for agitated patients who need to calm down. Complicating his prescription was the fact that two days earlier I had been given an amphetamine shot. I didn't know what it was and learned later that it was what the kids on the street called speed. It was supposed to help me out of my depression. It did, temporarily. I talked non-stop for several hours after the shot, but when the drug wore off, I was back in my black hole. The next day I was given Thorazine. I was severely depressed, barely able to move or eat and now on Thorazine.

Second day of Thorazine, I could not get out of bed. The nurse came in to give me yet another dose of the Big T and chastised me for still being in bed. I struggled up and staggered across the hall to the bathroom. Sitting on the toilet I felt the life leaving my body. I got on my knees, crawled to the hallway and said "I need help." Then everything went black. All of my organs had stopped working. I was no longer breathing and had no pulse. I was clinically dead. My psychiatrist jammed an adrenaline filled needle into my arm, and then called for help from the other building.

Help came in the form of an Internist who didn't believe in psychiatry, yet he often was on call and worked in psychiatric hospitals. He was the person who explained to me about the inadvisability of giving a patient an amphetamine one day and Thorazine the next. The psychiatric community trusted him because they knew he would relentlessly search for a physical cause until he was certain none existed. He began CPR to try to get my heart started. "Did you save up your pills?" someone yelled. I heard this coming from a great distance and managed to say no just before losing consciousness. For the second time, I was clinically dead.

I left my body. It was strange, floating around near the ceiling watching everything they were doing and saying. I felt peaceful, calm, and curious, but not afraid. I saw my bathrobe wide open and a voice in my head shouted, "Get back in there and zip up that bathrobe!" Catholic upbringing to the rescue! I returned to my body just as the nurse was saying, "I thought she was dead." I recall asking the nurse, "Please zipper up my bathrobe." She seemed puzzled that I knew it was open.

The diagnosis was Addison's disease. My adrenal glands were not functioning. They treated me with steroids. The internist told me my hospital records state that "the patient suddenly collapsed and was transferred to Christ Hospital by ambulance, condition looked poor." There was nothing sudden about it; I had been trying for weeks to tell them I needed medical attention. After a few days in the intensive care unit of Christ Hospital and a few additional days in their psychiatric ward having a variety of diagnostic tests done, it was back to Cauldhill Barnett to recover from both my mental illness and the recent trauma.

Twenty years passed before I told anyone about my experience of leaving my body. The experience did not make any kind of sense to me until much later. In retrospect, I realize that it propelled me to begin taking my recovery into my own hands. I believe that experience also laid groundwork and prepared me for what was to come in my Spiritual life journey.

I remember the day I finally went home to stay in 1972, nearly two years after my initial hospitalization. The recognition came in a flash, and I just knew I had to go right then or I might never go. I left group therapy, packed up my car, said goodbye to a few friends and headed for home. Like a mama bear that will go after anyone who threatens her cubs, I pushed away my friend who tried to talk me out of leaving that day. I was going home to take care of my children; stay out of my way.

I signed myself out of the hospital and went home knowing my psychiatrist would take care of the proper paperwork the next day. I knew with certainty that I would not be back to stay. The hospital had gotten me back to the ability to function and my intuition worked to send me home. My last admission, the one including Christ Hospital was three months in length.

The time at the hospital was quite an education. Some might even call it an adventure. Not an adventure one would choose to repeat, I admit, but it seemed to fit the path my life was taking. As William Styron said so well when he wrote about his own descent into madness, "For, in fact, the hospital was my salvation...I found the repose, the assuagement of the tempest in my brain, that I was unable to find in my quiet farmhouse."

In 1973 when we were living in College Hill, Ohio, Bruce and I moved our furniture into a small house we had just purchased where Elizabeth, now age nine, Jane, six and Emma, three, would live with me. Our divorce came as a result of how different I was following my experiences in the hospital. For the eleven years of our marriage, I had been willing to do Bruce's bidding. He insisted on having his way in all matters and I was mostly afraid. I never bought a piece of clothing without his approval. One time after being home from the hospital a while, I went shopping and bought an "up to date" outfit, but when I put it on, he said, "it's okay, just don't wear it any time you are with me." I took the outfit back. It was the last time I took anything back that I really liked.

Right after that incident, I looked at other things in our marriage and knew I could no longer live as we had been. I had become stronger, more independent and was on my way to total health. Our marriage could not survive how I had changed.

We would do what was best for our children. We were to stay friends and used the same lawyer to negotiate the terms of our divorce. Sister Alice was once again a strong support for the children and me when Bruce and I divorced. As I struggled being a single Mom, Alice was there, helping me to see the good in what I was doing and helping me to be there for the girls. The decision to divorce was not easy, but I knew that the woman Bruce had married no longer existed and was only going to change more in the future.

CHAPTER FIVE

WAKING UP

About a year after my divorce, at the age of thirty-four, I was lying in a hospital bed after surgery to remove my uterus. I was in a great deal of pain. The Catholic priest who was assigned to that hospital asked; "Would you like me to bring you communion tomorrow?" "No thank you," I replied in a very small voice.

For the first time in my life, I refused communion, at that time, the cornerstone of my religious life. It had been there since childhood. It was now time for me to move on and find my own spiritual life. I was newly divorced and beginning to raise my three daughters on my own. Questions regarding my Catholicism had risen for what I thought were practical reasons. How do I remain in a church as a divorced woman when that church does not recognize divorce? And there were philosophical and emotional reasons. *How* do I learn to live with the church's teachings about chastity and still have a healthy sexual life with a new partner?

"Well," the priest said in an angry tone, "I'll come by and give you my blessing, unless you don't want that either!" I felt as if someone had slammed a heavy brick into me and I was sinking into the bed. I could not move or respond. I felt numb, then pain from his chastising, and then the tears came and stayed with me for most of the night.

The next morning the pain eased a bit and this man's total lack of compassion hit me. I was furious. To the nurse on duty, I exclaimed, "It says here on this form if you want to see a clergy person you should let the nurse know. If I never want to see that priest again, do I also let you know? In fact, can you get word to him that if he ever darkens my door again, I will throw this water pitcher at him?"

What a revelation. I could get angry at a priest and nothing would happen to me. Though I had struggled with many of the tenets of the Catholic Church, this was the first time I had ever been consciously angry at a priest. Previously, nothing had shaken the underlying respect I was taught to have for the clergy. Surely, I had been sleep walking all those years, following without question what I had been told as a child.

As if in some Rip Van Winkle effect, I woke from years of sleeping and looked at the world in a new way. I was the only one who could make decisions of spiritual importance in my life. I did not leave the Catholic Church immediately after this experience, but I began to look at other ways of being. Leaving the church helped me embrace my recovery and healing.

I joined Parents without Partners (PWP), a diverse group of men and women raising their children as single parents. I met other Catholics who were struggling with similar questions about the church. This group gave me people who shared my concerns. On Sundays, we made it a point to have activities that involved bringing our children together. The first time the four of us went to a Sunday picnic with this group Jane asked, "You mean all of these kids only live with one of their parents?" "Yes," I assured her. This was the beginning of helping my children not feel so strange living just with their mother.

For me this group was my spiritual community; we showed love to each other and to each other's children. Comfort, love, and special friendships forged during this time gave rise to feelings of spiritual wellness. I could not have expressed it in this way at first, but I felt supported and cared for. This became our 'church,' if you will.

At a PWP gathering I met a most amazing woman. Roberta Hunt, affectionately known as Boe, became a close friend in the moment that we met. We looked across the room at each other and before we even spoke both of us laughed and gave each other the thumbs up signal. There was something in our connection that we both knew was special. Boe was a loving, caring friend and confidant for 40 years. Ours was a friendship that could endure all of the changes that were to come in my life. Boe and I were both aware that our friendship was sustaining each of us.

Shortly after joining PWP, I began dating. Some of the men I dated were part of this organization and some I met other places such as the Folk Song Society I belonged to.

Parents without Partners brought lots of singing around camp fires with family and friends. Harmony showed up at all sorts of places, especially the local coffee house. Ohio was the place I first sang publicly. Leo Coffee house in Clifton, Ohio held an Open Mic every Sunday night. I often went there with my children. Everyone who was interested was encouraged to take a turn at singing on the Open Mic nights. I did this for several years in a row with wonderful support from the local musicians. I felt joyful and grateful.

Again, Sister Alice supported me during these times. One of her greatest gifts is the ability to see what is good in everyone no matter what their current struggles might be. She saw me through my days in PWP and lent support so often during my time with various boyfriends. I never had the feeling Alice was rolling her eyes at me, even though later I certainly did some rolling of my own eyes at my own single mom adventures.

Looking inward for answers to life's questions broadened my perspectives. I had made some serious decisions up to this point, but always with a sense of good old fashion Catholic Guilt. The choices to divorce the father of my children and have a boyfriend came with their share of guilt, though I felt certain they were choices I had to make. Maybe, the real reason for my anger toward the priest was that his actions forced me to look at the guilt I was feeling.

Over time I became grateful to my friend

the Catholic priest and his clumsy way of being. He did me a favor. I began to look at myself in a more honest manner. I woke up and made decisions much more consciously going forward. The transformation did not happen overnight, but the insult was the catalyst to begin a new way of living. So, here's to Father what's-his-name, whoever and wherever he may be. Thank you for being a pain in my ass and helping me to see.

This was the beginning of an understanding that I would be looking for new ways of spiritual being in the world. It was to be a few more years before I began my search in earnest. In 1976, Mom was diagnosed with Cancer, which took my heart and spirit energy while she made her transition.

CHAPTER SIX

DEATH WITH DIGNITY

Proverbs 31:25:

She is clothed with strength and dignity;
she can laugh at the days to come.

In 1976, my mother Victoria, now a tall, stately 79, walked down the hallway of the hospital with her head held high, shoulders back, and a calm look on her face. A sense of dignity emanated from her. It was the day after her left breast had been removed due to cancer, and it was important to her that she get back to the business of life and look elegant to boot!

After returning home from the hospital she had some chemotherapy and was considered cancer free for the next year and a half. There was little talk about it; only that someone made sure she had her regular checkups while she was busy visiting and exchanging family gossip with her sister, May.

During a checkup about a year and a half after her surgery, cancer was found in two other places in her body. "That's it," she said, "they only get one shot at me and they've had that. There will be no more treatment, it's time to stop."

She moved through her demise with all the grace possible. The cancer took its toll. After several months passed, she would call Bethany and ask to be taken for new dresses, saying, "These dresses are way too big for me now and I cannot go out looking like this."

During my last visit before her death, I found a bottle of medicine in her refrigerator. "Mom, what is this for?"

"Oh, its chemotherapy, I get it filled every once in a while, because it makes the doctors feel better if they think I am taking it. It makes me nauseous; I should take that for another six months so I can feel sick and live for another six months? I'm 81 years old—if I wasn't dying of cancer, I'd be dying of something else."

We both laughed at that point and I said, "I don't give a shit how old you are, you're my mother, you are not supposed to die," which made us laugh and cry at the same time. I was 38 and felt so young to be losing my mother. As I left her to go back to Ohio, she said to me, "Oh my God, Dottie, it is so much fun when you are around." I will always cherish that moment.

Elizabeth and I went to Boston for Mom's last few days. On November 4, 1978, the hospital sent word to my sister Bethany to call the family; it was time. As each of us arrived, we made sure to tell Mom we were there. I took her hand and began to sing "Peace is Flowing like a River." At first the words hardly came out of my mouth— the lump in my throat hurt. But slowly they came. Martha, Lydia and Bethany joined in a little at first and then slowly grew stronger. Many of us sang to her the last three hours of her life. We knew she could hear us even though she no longer talked.

Her wishes were well known. There was to be no treatment except for comfort care. This included no intravenous for hydration or nourishment. She died surrounded by all her sons and daughters, in laws, outlaws, many grandchildren and her sister and niece.

In the end, her rule was law; in the end she came into her power. Her strength never ebbed in terms of knowing what was right for her and how she wanted to die.

MOM

Mom – with her fears so well hidden
    beneath the stoic exterior
Mom – with her wonderful way
    of laughing
Mom – with her sense of timing
    around death
We had some last laughs together
We had some first tears together
Mom – constantly talking to herself
    in a whisper so we wouldn't notice
Mom – I think I understand now.

The grieving began for me when I was able to go the next day and find a place to scream. I sat up on the hill on the playground across from the grammar school where I went as a child. I screamed at the top of my lungs, like the whole world could hear me. Apparently, some of them did. I saw a police car coming up the street and I thought, *something must be wrong at the school!* Then, *oh* no he is turning into where I am...

I told him why I had been screaming. He said, "It is okay."

On his two-way radio, I overhear: "What's happening Joe?"

"It's okay."

"What's happening?"

"I'll tell you later."

I wished the ground would open up under me even though I had done what I needed to do. I thought for sure I was far enough away from all the houses that no one would hear me.

I told my brother Stephen about the incident later at Bethany's. He laughed a lot and said, "You gave the guys at the station something to laugh about. They probably could use that."

Stephen used it too. He told the story over and over at the wake. Laughter was how he handled his grief. So, my little episode at the playground was a gift to him and a healing for me.

God's Will

As if some god had done this to her

As if she hadn't chosen to go--- this way

at this time-- with all these people around her.

As if she hadn't taken her power at last.

Afterwards –

Sitting on the hill across from my old school

like when I was a kid

Screaming, screaming at the top of my lungs

not…like when I was a kid

Like the whole world could hear me

And some of them did

MOVING FROM SURVIVING TO THRIVING

In 1979, I married my second husband, Frank, and moved my family from Ohio to Morristown, New Jersey. It was not on my list of things to do that year. Frank and I had been dating for about a year, having met at the Folk Song Society of Greater Cincinnati which was the biggest reason to being dating. Though we enjoyed the same kinds of music and some adventurous backpacking and cross-country skiing together, marriage was not in the picture for us. However, Frank's company had asked him to move to New Jersey and he didn't want to go alone. That was about the only reason to do this that we knew of. So why did I say yes? I was a single parent, had the most amazing group of friends, my children settled in schools, and a job I loved; I had begun my studies at the University of Cincinnati. In those days I had not yet learned how to ask for guidance from my soul or from the Divine, which is how I refer to the Source that connects us all. As if in a dream it came to me to do this, I said yes.

At the University of Cincinnati Medical Center Libraries, where I was working at the time, I had a friend; Susan, whom I knew wouldn't judge me. We were sitting at break one day and I asked Susan, "Can I just tell you something a bit strange?" "I have no idea why I am marrying Frank. I only know that I am supposed to go to New Jersey and he is the way to get there." And so, it went. We married, moved our families, my three daughters and his son, bought a huge house and began living together.

Two weeks after we moved into our new home, Frank was diagnosed with melanoma. His physician, whom I had never met, called me and told me my husband had about six months to live, and what's more, "He doesn't know how serious this is, so you cannot tell him. He is going to be coming home, will get his affairs in order and will likely die soon. He may not be ready to face this so we have not told him." I was so shocked that it never occurred to me to ask him why he was going to get his affairs in order if he did not know the prognosis of his diagnosis.

I was completely devastated. It felt like being caught in the undercurrent of a huge wave in the ocean; I couldn't get my head above the water. What do I do? I know no one here, have no close friends, and have my three daughters; ages nine, twelve and fifteen, plus his son, thirteen, to be concerned about. At the local Community College Counseling Center, I found a counselor to talk to. She helped me keep myself together, during those early days, to take care of my family. I realized she was not going to be the long-term therapist that I felt I needed, and, in fact, she was the first person I asked about helping me find another.

In Cincinnati I had seen, for a short time, a Bioenergetics therapist. Bioenergetics' Analysis is a body-centered psychotherapy. Body centered psychotherapy works in a way that pure talk therapy cannot. Why? Trauma that happens to us is stored in the cells of our body – not our brain. The memories must be uncovered to heal, hence the total dead feeling in my body at the beginning of my work with Eli. In order not to feel or be in touch with the trauma memories, I had to shut down all feeling in my body. Shutting down was a way to keep the memories at bay. By working directly with the body to relieve tensions and release blocked expression, body centered therapy allowed me to access the underlying cause of my illness.

I liked this way of working in therapy so I asked the Counseling Center plus two other sources for a referral to a Bioenergetics Therapist. They gave me Eli Rubin's name. It took more than a year to begin seeing him. I had no idea then that I would spend the next eight years doing very difficult, very worthwhile therapy with Eli. We met once a week for most of that time and twice a week for three of those years. It was a brutal, difficult process. Eli was able to confront me when appropriate and be incredibly kind and gentle when that was called for.

In the beginning, the work made no sense to me, but I knew I was in the right place. In our early sessions together, Eli would ask me to stand up, but on only one leg. After a brief time, I would say, "I need to sit down or change legs, my leg hurts too much."

"Keep standing," was his reply.

After what seemed like another ten minutes, I would say, "Eli, I have to sit down, my leg is in so much pain I'm afraid I will fall."

"I don't see any pain in your face. I hear the words you are saying, but they don't match the expression on your face. It's okay to sit down."

We did variations of this exercise as part of our sessions for many months, perhaps even a year, before the pain in my body reached my face. Eli was helping me to get in touch with my body. He was showing me that I was totally disconnected from what my body was feeling most of the time. Gradually I actually began to *feel* the pain.

In 1982, after I had begun working with Eli, Frank's melanoma was declared cured by the doctors. Frank, our children and I celebrated together. We took some great family vacations at the Jersey shore. The vacations included all six of us, Emma, age eleven, Jane, fourteen, Frank's son, sixteen and Elizabeth, seventeen. They were lively and fun times. At times, Frank was very supportive of my therapy and I felt we had a marriage that was good. Other times Frank resented my work with Eli and the amount of my attention it took. We had many ups and downs during those years.

We joined the local Unitarian Fellowship in Morristown. It was there that I began to look in earnest for new ways of spiritual being. I joined several women's groups. The groups studied together and met on a regular basis. We gathered on the Friday nearest to the full moon every month and led each other in rituals of healing, the seasons, and honoring the Goddess in every woman.

In my search for a new way, one of the first books that came across my path was Starhawk's "Dreaming the Dark." It was my introduction to pagan rituals. The rituals I practice today come through my own knowing and through experiences I've had with fellow practicing pagans. In Dreaming the Dark, Starhawk speaks of the Goddess in each person; "the Goddess as birth-giver, weaver, earth and growing plant, wind and ocean, flame, web, moon and milk, all speak to me of the powers of connectedness, sustenance, healing, creating." I sought out workshops and weekend retreats that Starhawk was leading. She became my mentor in the practice of Witchcraft and my beginning spiritual emergence.

Paganism and my tradition of Witchcraft in particular use ritual to express religious experience and is grounded in peaceful and healing ways of being honoring the power from within each individual. With permission, I draw on my daughter Emma's philosophy of Witchcraft, as it so closely aligns with mine: "I believe that the divine is manifest in every person, animal, plant and the earth. I feel the presence of the divine in the earth. I honor and connect to the divine in the practice of the Craft and pagan ritual, like celebrating the earth's changing seasons."

The rituals replenish the energy I need to move through life. During my many years of healing, ritual became the cornerstone of my life. For me today, as a practicing Witch, uplifting energy and ritual are a daily part of life. I begin each day greeting and giving thanks for Mother Earth, air, fire, water and the Divine beings as they manifest within me. These five elements are considered sacred to most pagans and to the Craft. I now know that some of the rituals I took part in during my formative years with the Catholic Church were helpful to me also, most especially the music.

In Margo Adler's book "Drawing Down the Moon," she speaks of one of the major tenants of Witchcraft and other pagan paths: "And *it harm none, do what ye will*". Learning and studying about earth-centered religions opened my eyes to the goodness in everyone. It was instrumental in my ability to stay with the years of therapy I needed to become whole. It gave me tools to work with.

In August 1983, Frank was diagnosed with multiple myeloma. The new diagnosis was a destructive cancer of the bone marrow, and the doctor told us it was scattered throughout his body. There were already holes in his bones in several places. I watched him shrink in front of my eyes in a very short time. It was now, only a matter of time till he died. Frank never acknowledged to me, or anyone else, that he was, in fact, dying.

Repeating the pattern of the first bout of cancer, he had good times and sick times. My vacations were spent mostly taking care of him during his sick times. His vacations were spent going camping with his friends, and this time, coming home with tales of his adventures, as he called them, with another woman. It became obvious to me that keeping this marriage together was probably not going to be an option. We simply did not agree on what was the appropriate way for a husband and wife team to behave.

Our marriage, along with my husband's body, was falling apart. I did my best to focus my help on the children and their lives. I felt frightened, lost and fragile most of the time. Eli helped me to function and keep going. One day I said to Eli through my tears, "I can't even stand alone. I am hanging onto you for dear life!" His response: "Well, at least you still think life is dear."

I was angry and felt used because I could not take fun time off because of having to take care of Frank during his down times. I found ways to deal with my frustration about our marriage that were very unhealthy. Having a flirtation with one of my fellow workers was one way to distract myself from the feeling of betrayal. What a charade! It was Eli who pointed out to me what I was doing and what my husband was doing by camping with his woman friend. And that my life could only get better for me if I changed my behavior.

It seems important to mention that Frank did not change after we married. I knew he had a penchant for doing what he wanted for fun or adventure, that he believed in Open Marriage and although I was clear that was not what I wanted, I married him anyway. Such a cliché I was, in refusing to look at who he really was and thinking things would be different. In fact, keeping our marriage together became impossible when I did change. With enough hard work and willingness to face our own foibles, I believe we can change our ways of being in the world. I filed for divorce. Our divorce became final in 1985 and Frank moved out of our home. Divorcing a dying man was the single most difficult thing I have ever done in my life. I was more able to be supportive to him when he was no longer disruptive to my life and my family. Frank lived about a year and a half after we stopped living together.

Eli and I worked together for four additional years after my divorce. Eli was with me in so many ways during those years of struggle encouraging me to keep going and not give up. When I needed nurturing, he was there in a gentle way. When I needed a kick in the ass he obliged. I began to listen to and pay attention to what my physical feelings were telling me, and to my psychic and spiritual pain as well. I became a professional crier and still am to this day. It was wrenching, torrential crying often accompanied by severe pain almost too hard to bear at times. I speak of it as a matter of fact now, but at the time it was brutal to go through. Often, most individuals are afraid that if we start crying, we will never stop. My experience was that long bouts of crying released so much of my pain that I had more room for life giving feelings. Eli had a sign on the wall of his office. It said simply: "It always stops raining."

The following dreams had come early in my work with Eli and on the same day.

Seems I have two ways to go to work. One requires making a lot of adjustments. One requires leaving things the same and it is up to me to decide which way to go. Making all the changes is such a pain, but seems to be the way I've chosen.

I picked up a hitchhiker. He got me though part of a massive traffic jam and he was going to help me get through the rest. I felt I had to pick him up. He tried to talk to me. I pretended I didn't know how to talk. I started using a bogus sign language. He understood sign language and started talking to me with his hands. I was forced to talk, to tell him I didn't understand sign language. "So, you can talk," he said. I felt trapped. Where can I let this guy off? I don't want him in my car.

Part of the work I did with Eli centered on my dreams. I brought them to sessions and Eli helped me to see what the dreams were showing me. Some of them were quite obvious to me, but most required Eli asking the right questions in order for me to see what the message was. I believe that a good deal of the time, dreams give symbolic messages. Understanding what the symbols meant helped us to focus on what was going on in my life at the moment. I was quite methodical about keeping dreams written down. I kept a book beside my bed to write in the minute I woke. Later, I would type them up on pieces of paper to take to therapy. Like a water faucet has been turned off, when either Eli or I was out of town and treatment ceased, the dreams stopped. It was interesting to me that as soon as therapy started again, the dreams came back. I felt my unconscious was leading the way to healing.

There were times when the work we did frightened the hell out of me. I would barely be able to get myself to Eli's office the fear was so great. Being confronted with all my demons and the transference feelings; that is, unconscious positive or negative feelings directed toward therapist, I had directed to Eli was very scary.

I'm trying to get back home, but I have to go through a large body of water to get there. I'm afraid of drowning. I don't swim very well. I don't know where I am, but I seem to be almost surrounded by salt water. There is someone else with me trying to tell me it's OK to go through this – that I'll get to the other side. But I cannot see where I'm going.

In many therapeutic models, water represents emotions. Clearly, I was on a roller coaster ride during these years. Fear was prevalent, but sadness and anger were also present. At home there were times when I cried for hours or threw up on a regular basis, which I found out is a good way to release fear from your body. It was painful, but I knew I had to keep going.

I had the following conversation with Eli on the phone one day when I was freaking out. I had awakened that day with a headache that felt like the top of my head wanted to come off and was in a panic.

"Eli" I said, "I feel like I am falling apart."

"You are Dot", he replied. "That's what is supposed to happen. It is the only way to build a healthy self. This might be a good time to start coming to therapy twice a week."

It was such a relief just to hear him say that falling apart was expected. It was what was supposed to happen if I were to heal. The following dream came about half way through my years with Eli. This dream felt like the birth canal. I was definitely birthing a new life with a prolonged delivery then.

I was trying to get out through a tube-like chute. I thought it was a staircase, but it turned out to be a narrow tube that curved at the bottom to go around a corner and out. I could not see exactly how to get out.

Sometimes during those years, I was filled with rage causing my whole body to shake. Eli taught me how to release the anger by using a tennis racket to beat a pillow or two on my bed. I learned to let out the anger safely through movement, loud yelling and name calling. At home I put music on in my bedroom to help drown out the noise. I told my children what I was going to do, giving them the opportunity to go to visit friends who lived close by.

Years later, Jane told me, "We would invite our friends in and all go down the basement and dance to the rhythm of you beating the bed." Leave it to children to find an ingenious way to cope with a mother who was acting deranged. I knew what I was doing was for the best for myself and my children. It was a way to become healthy and more vibrantly alive.

I managed to keep my administrative job and somehow keep the house working during these years. Eventually I made a decision to quit my job, get a loan on the house and go to school full-time to finish my degree while still working and healing with Eli. I graduated from Kean College, Union New Jersey in 1988.

Working with my body as well as my mind

helped me to uncover the memories of my early abusive years and clear the pain of them from my body and soul. I thought that I might not be believed when I revealed the contents of my memories; Eli assured me that my expressions and crying out while I was remembering what happened to me as a child could not be faked. What I was feeling was real and very frightening. At times I was afraid I would die if I remembered any more. That somehow the memories would be the death of me. Without knowing what my memories would be, Eli assured me that "if you survived and lived through the events happening, you will live through the remembering."

Someone came in my bedroom window – walked across the room towards me and tried to strangle me. I was screaming and kicking my feet. I could not stop him from coming. I screamed louder, kicking very hard...

I woke up, still screaming and kicking.

Everyone living in the house, Jane, Emma and my roommate and friend Donna had heard me and rushed into my bedroom to wake me up. This dream came very shortly after the memories of how my father had tried to smother me with the blanket when I was a child. It was not unusual for abuse memories to come as dreams, usually after there had been some uncovering of what had been repressed so many years before.

It was gentle work on Eli's part, though the memories did not feel gentle and I kicked my legs and screamed, "No. No. No..." over and over. We did this part of our work together until I could speak the words about my abuse without choking and without being afraid, I would die. The timing of this work, that is, how long we worked on this very traumatic part of my healing is difficult to remember. Wonder of wonders. How long isn't important.

Sometime in my last year with Eli, I told him that I had been accepted into a graduate school program in Keene, New Hampshire. I paused for a moment and asked, "Why am I telling you this?"

"I expect this means you will be leaving me and moving on."

Softly, in a puzzled voice, "I guess I am!"

Saying goodbye took several months. This leave-taking was a scenario that I could not have even imagined just a few months earlier. After working with Eli for eight years, I realized that this vital relationship was, up to that point, the most important relationship I had ever had. I credit Eli with helping me to save my life.

Like a ship trying to find its way through fog, I played out this leave-taking not really seeing what I was gearing up to do. We spoke about my leaving several more times before I was ready to depart and agreed to do short phone sessions after I got to New Hampshire to help ease the transition. I was afraid, but there was no holding me back. My discomfort about this move was evident in the following dream.

Driving south on the highway late at night. It is very

foggy and I cannot see very far in front of me. Only distant lights of oncoming cars or cars that pass me help me to have any sense of the distance. It's like I'm driving on blind faith. I know it's OK for a little bit in front of me, but I just have to trust that the road is still there ahead of the light. And will be there when it comes time to change lanes so I can make the turn-off. I'm very frightened – not at all certain it is safe to change lanes – but I can no longer stay where I am now. I am aware I would just keep going forever but never get where I want to be. I keep watching the other lane to check traffic, telling myself, "You must move – go now – no one's going to come smashing into the back of you – you would at least see some light if there was something coming your way.

On the same morning, another dream came as the words to a Harry Chapin song: *I'm going nowhere, and anywhere's a better place to be.*

Eli had in his office a glass Eskimo paper weight that I had always admired. During a particularly vulnerable time, Eli gave it to me to hold until he returned from a vacation. It helped. As I was saying my final goodbye in-person, Eli gave me the Eskimo to take with me. I was a bit mystified and very grateful for this gesture. "Someday, when you no longer need it, you'll send it back to me," he said smiling, "if I live that long." It was his warm parting gift and greeting. Thank you.

That was in May 1990. June 2015. I was ready to send it back, but found out that Eli Rubin left this planet a few years before. I am sad he is no longer with us. I guess the Eskimo is to stay with me. When I left Eli, I was choosing life-affirming ways to live my life. In 1991 I dedicated my book of poetry to him, saying, "To Eli, who was willing to be a pain in my ass, so that together, we could heal the pain of my Spirit."

I now know Eli Rubin was the reason I had to go to New Jersey.

CHAPTER EIGHT

SPIRITUAL AWAKENING

In 1990, I moved to New Hampshire to live alone for the first time in my life. I had been through the difficult years of my daughters going off to college and leaving me. They were not easy experiences. I cried for long periods of time after each of them moved on to do the work they needed for their lives. My life up to that point had been about raising my children while doing therapy that helped me to take care of my family. There was emptiness within even though I knew they had not really left me in total. Grief showed its head again. It comes in so many forms. Moving through the uncovered emotions and grieving the loss of my childhood helped me to understand the grief I felt as my children left home to make their way.

Elizabeth had gone to Arizona to finish her college years and made the decision to make Phoenix her home. Jane graduated from Rutgers University and moved up to the Boston area about the same time I moved to New Hampshire, and Emma finished her college years in Washington, D.C., staying on there until she got a job in Eastern Europe soon after graduation.

Soon after my arrival, I sought out a new therapist, Helen. The friend that recommended her told me that she was known for her hands-on energy work approach to therapy. I began seeing her as a client in September 1990. She and Eli, my New Jersey therapist, met through a phone conversation to help with my transition. Eli assured me that he felt she was a grounded therapist. That was the beginning of an 18-year therapeutic relationship with Helen. She became my therapist, teacher, mentor and friend. The transition to working with her, in a sense, seemed like a cosmic conveyor belt, a well-oiled machine designed to move me through my life journey. With rare, loving care Helen guided me through those years, whether as therapist, mentor, or friend. I am indebted to her for much of my well-being.

I had never experienced energy work prior to this and so the old cliché *nothing ventured, nothing gained* described how I felt when making the decision to begin work with Helen. The very first time I had a session with her, my attitude changed. I was sure this was exactly where I needed to be.

In the beginning I didn't know what to expect, and, as time went on, I still didn't know what to expect! Many surprises arrived as our work progressed, but we continued.

Energy work involves the client lying on a healing table, while the practitioner's hands touch the person's body in the places they are drawn to. Each session has its own life. I developed the ability to close my eyes and look inside my body for signs that would help me understand the feelings arising at any particular time. Most often the signs I saw were pictures. One time I, feeling devastatingly sad, looked inside and saw myself as a very small child crying in a crib. The scene gave me a sense of being totally alone with no one to care for me. During this therapy we would talk, with me doing most of the talking, while also feeling the energy changes moving as Helen's hands moved moment by moment.

In July, 1991 I was lying on a healing table in Helen's working room. She had her hands on my body near my hips and near the base of my spine. With my eyes closed, I saw and felt what looked to me like a round black ball, about the size of a golf ball or a little larger, at the base of my spine. It felt heavy. I watched within me and felt it move up my spine, through my entire body, and out my mouth. A sound came out of my mouth that was loud enough that it could have been the sound of the ball. I knew the two were connected. Helen's hands followed the course of the ball as it moved. I stared at her.

"What the hell was that?" I blurted.

"Is that the first time you have ever moved Kundalini?"

"What the hell is that?" I questioned, feeling totally shaken.

My spiritual emergence began in earnest with the awakening of the Kundalini. I describe Kundalini as the life force energy that sits at the base of the spine of human beings. It is well known and accepted in Eastern religions and cultures, but not as well known in the Western world. I learned from my studies and from my personal experience that when Kundalini begins to move through your body, it helps to clear out stuck energy places. It can also move previously stored trauma to promote healing. After that first experience, I came to know that sound plays a large role in the movement of Kundalini.

Kundalini continued to move for the next three years. The process can be explained as fascinating and enriching, but certainly not fun. My experiences with the Kundalini movement included long nights of periodic vomiting, excess energy and too little sleep. Along with these difficulties, memories came flooding back. I shed heaps of tears. I saw memories which I once thought were hallucinations. My wondrous ability to survive my childhood by suppressing memories too difficult for a child's mind amazed me. It was remarkable that I instinctively found ways to cope with, and keep at bay, these very difficult memories. My father's brutal treatment of me as a child had begun to surface in my last years with Eli. Helen's energy work brought another layer and more details of the abuse to my conscious mind and to my body, allowing more healing to happen.

There are so many parts of me. I feel scattered all over the place. I'm not sure which one of me is operating at any given time. I need to put all the parts together to be whole.

This dream came to me early in my work with Helen. It was telling me that there was more work to be done. During energy work, the practitioner feels stuck places or movement in the body that they can then ask the client about during sessions. These exchanges helped me to pay attention to the slightest change within my body. Helen often knew what to ask me because of the subtle changes in my energy field. Her questions would bring forth what was happening inside. The work was difficult in that, once again, I was terrified by what was coming to the surface concerning my early abuse years. Kicking my legs on the table and loud screaming went with these sessions. Clearing out another layer of my trauma was leading me to wholeness, though at times I was hard pressed to see how. Nothing deterred me from staying with the process. I knew this was the work that my soul needed at this time.

During two of the years Helen and I worked together, I attended a psychology graduate school program, which included going to weekly classes and weekend workshops and working in my prescribed internship. Kundalini experiences sometimes made keeping up with all the requirements of my graduate work very challenging.

One day in the middle of listening to a presentation at an Internship workshop, I began to feel energy moving low in my body. I got out of the room and asked for a glass of orange juice, hoping to keep it at bay until I could get safely out of the building. This was not to be. I found a spot to lie on the floor because I knew I would fall if I did not get down. My whole body began to move in several directions of its own volition. My arms and legs were flopping on both sides. The trunk of my body was moving swiftly back and forth in very quick motions. After a few minutes, the movement stopped.

I looked up and there were two staff women from the Mental Health Center standing by with frightened looks on their faces. I assured them, "I am not having a seizure!" I'm sure they didn't know what to think.

"I have to get up and go to the bathroom."
"No, don't do that – wait for the ambulance."
"I'm getting up and going!" I knew my colon was about to empty out and no one was stopping me. I got up and headed into the bathroom.
"We are coming with you!"
"Enter at your own risk!" I warned them. They did and we all managed to get through that moment.

I was trying to find my way back from a hospital in a strange city and hotel. It was hard to find my way back. I got into the elevator. I pressed the button for one floor up. There was padding on the walls like a freight elevator. It was small, I sat down. The elevator was narrower at the top. The doors closed and it moved and then stopped, "Oh, no" I thought "I'm stuck. Don't panic. There are no buttons to push for help – how much air is in here? Will anyone ever find me? I mustn't panic. – have to breathe." My dream-self thought, "at last, a padded cell!'

Even in my sleep, I have a sense of humor.

Early on, Helen suggested that my heart was armored with a protective shield around it. I knew she was right. Only recently had I uncovered memories of my father and the memories were still frightening. Helen could feel that I held a lot in the base of my spine, and no wonder, considering a good deal of the trauma happened in that area. We uncovered more about my abuse and the turns it took. I kicked, screamed, and yelled during our sessions. Over and over I kicked away the vestiges of trauma that still hid within my body and psyche. I was determined to get to a place of feeling safe. Although I was often frightened, angry and exhausted, we worked like this for nearly a year in weekly sessions prior to the onset of my Kundalini awakening. Kundalini movement propelled me to keep moving the trauma out of my body and allowed for my Divine presence to speak to me. Working with Helen was a many-faceted process.

I was watching myself from another dimension. I had two bodies – one in this world, one on a higher plane – as if I were an ascended being. It seemed very real, almost like I had a guardian angel except both bodies were me.

This dream was a reminder to me of my near-death experience in the psychiatric hospital. It had been twenty years since that incident and Helen was the first person, I ever told about it. The fact that I knew, and never forgot, that experience helped me to move through other unexpected difficulties that came with Kundalini rising and with out-of-body experiences.

One day, while I was on the table, I felt thickness, a heavy darkness in my head. The energy moved down through me and out my legs. As I looked inside, I saw a black tornado swirling; it moved down my leg. I had pains and pins and needles in my left leg. In my back was a small sharp point, about one and a half inches deep, like the head of an arrow or bullet. I closed my eyes and looked into my body to see where it came from. I saw myself in chains being dragged—in a ragged dress. It felt like a heavy, dark time. A man with iron on his arms, carrying a club with spokes, coming out of the tornado, began yelling in my left ear that I wasn't moving fast enough. I was a witch being taken away for healing people. The man hit me with club. Lead stuck in my back and I fell to the ground. He put his foot on my neck and crushed it to ground. It felt like I was choking. I began to choke on the table. My face became older than my actual age at the time. My face turned into a long narrow face with brown hair and some gray. Helen said my face changed when I saw the face of the woman from back then.

I understand this to mean that healing work has been a part of me for more than one lifetime.

About three years into our time together, Helen told me that she learned to do this work by working on her teacher, Ester, a healer in New Hampshire. She offered to teach me in the same manner if I was interested. I stopped breathing. It was a dream. I had wondered if I could learn to do this work.

"Are you okay Dorothea? Would you like to do this?" Helen asked.

"Yes," I replied.

"Okay, I just wondered because your heart stopped beating."

We both laughed.

Sometime after that conversation, our work moved back and forth between my being the client on the table and being the student and with Helen as the "client" on the table. Here are journal entries I wrote about this process.

May 1993: There was so much fear around working on Helen, "Do I know enough?" Helen was so easy with me. "Start with what you know" she encouraged. So, I did. I silently called in my guides, spirits or souls from other dimensions that sometimes speak to me, and Mary, Madeleine, St. Germane, angels, please be with me.

May 1993: I worked on Helen today for the first time. It was BIG... I felt the need to put my hands under her head. In my mind's eye, I saw a child being rocked and I sang "Oh, Mary don't you weep." After my initial nervousness, I knew I was totally there for her. Once our session stopped, I felt the shift right back to being Helen 's "pupil."

Late May 1993: It came to me to say a prayer just prior to working on anyone, and it is still with me today. The symbol that brings the prayer is two folded hands with wings of angels around me. The prayer is that I be with each person for their highest good, that I will let my own "stuff" be set aside. I ask that whatever comes to me either through feelings in my body or in my mind is about the person on the table – not me.

Early October, 1993: I worked on Helen for one hour today. It went really well, felt fine. Helen said, "You are good at this!" Wow! Coming from her that was quite a compliment.

Late October, I worked on Helen again. She said, "Your hands felt like they were in your Etheric body and your energy is like my Ester's. "Tom Harpur, in his book "The Uncommon Touch" explains that our Etheric body is an energy field that surrounds our physical body, sometimes called a personal aura. "Ester is around in spirit and she will work with you if you ask her to." Helen said. I had felt Ester's presence here in my house about two weeks prior. I evened out the energy in Helen's hips as it is very important that the client's energy field be as balanced as possible at the end of each session.

Some would say that all kind of lines were crossed in my relationship with Helen. These lines between personal and professional relationships are designated by the psychology community where I got my traditional training as a therapist. What I came to know through my work with Helen is that those lines are appropriate for individuals who are therapists that have not done this body-centered type of work on their own issues and are much more likely to let transference interfere. In our case, both Helen and I had spent many years healing our pasts. There were few dark shadows lingering.

Following graduate school, I began teaching psychology courses in two local colleges. I loved working with the students. Teaching was hard work, but I loved all the time I was involved in this part of my career life. At the same time, I began a private energy therapy practice in my home, grateful to have had and utilizing my training from graduate school and Helen.

At times, my sessions with Helen included time on her part being a supervisor. Even though my basic work came from my experiences with Helen, Kundalini awakening and my own healing, I saw that by listening to my inner spiritual being, I was shown how my work would differ from Helen 's. Early on in my practice, as my hands were on a woman client, an old 1950's sexist song kept coming into my head. I said several times to myself, I'm not singing that song to her! Like a nagging thought, the song would not go away. I told her, "there is a song in my head that will not go away and I think it needs to be sung for you."

"Okay, that will be fine," she agreed. As I sang the song to her she had a major break-through in her own healing process. The song had been part of a very difficult period in her life and hearing it allowed her to let go of some of the pain associated with that particular time.

After that experience, I no longer question songs that come to me during a session with a client. Once, a friend asked me, "Why don't you sing at local pubs as a way to earn some money?" I adamantly stated, "I don't want to use my music for work, but for pleasure." Little did I know what was to come in terms of using music in my work. In the years I learned to do hands-on energy work, I found songs coming into my head. Most often I don't know why a particular song is there, but often the client does. Whether they do or not, the information comes to me through their energy field and is not for me to judge, but just listen, pay attention, offer it and sing.

Having been raised in a traditional western world religion myself; I feel that this is an appropriate time in my story to speak about my current belief system to others with a similar background. Some readers may find the following information difficult, but I give this explanation here in the hopes that this will help each of you to keep an open mind as the story unfolds.

I came to believe, in those years of work with Helen and beyond, that all of us have within us an alliance of the human and the divine. For me the words universe, spirit, soul or essence represent that alliance. I use these words interchangeably. Some people reach a high spiritual vibration while on this planet. These beings are known in different cultures as Gurus, Mystics, Saints, Great Mothers, or the Divine. While here and after leaving this planet, they are available to people through their Spirits for religious guidance. When I speak of my guides, I am speaking of souls who have guided me from a different dimension. They have spoken to me on rare occasions and helped me understand what was going on. For me, my Spirit is the spark of the Divine within me. I believe the Divine is the highest spiritual vibration in existence. This vibration is referred to as God, Goddess or the Great Spirit or Love in many religious traditions.

Helen was the first person I had worked with who was guided by an Indian Guru, Neem Karoli Baba; some traditions might call him a mystic. He had lived on this planet until 1973, but his essence or spirit is available to us now. I developed my own work and relationship to Neem Karoli through training with Helen. In India, Maharajah, as he was affectionately called, was well known and, as Ram Dass says in his book Miracle of Love, "I recognized in him an alliance of the human and the divine." This is the alliance I refer to at the beginning of the above paragraph. Most especially I am indebted to Helen for bringing Neem Karoli Baba into my life and work.

For many years my dream for my life work had been to be a half-time college teacher and half-time therapist. I realized with wonder at some point in my last two years in New

Hampshire that I was living that dream. My life had profoundly changed. Helen and all of the other helpers during those many years, including a Women's Sacred Circle, were instrumental in bringing me through the recovery process to go on doing this work here and now with help from both sides of the veil.

CHAPTER NINE

THERAPEUTIC TOUCH (TT)

Beginning in 1992 soon after graduate school, I began my training as a Therapeutic Touch (TT) practitioner and teacher at Elliott Hospital, Manchester, New Hampshire. Therapeutic Touch is a healing modality that is scientifically based and many research studies can be found to back up its efficacy. The work I was learning from Helen is spiritually based energy work and relies on the practitioner first experiencing healing for herself on a deep level. The learner begins as the client in order to become clear enough to do this work. TT complemented the work I learned from Helen. The two different ways of working came together quite naturally; each reinforced the other. I also found that Therapeutic Touch was easier to introduce to clients as the treatments could be shorter in length. TT gradually helps clients wish to do the more spiritually-based work that comes with combining the two modalities that I offered.

When I first moved to New Hampshire in 1990, I took part in a brief introduction to Therapeutic Touch (TT) presented by two TT teachers. They spoke for a short time about the origins and creators of TT and then went on to guide the group in short energy exercises. The group paired up. We were instructed on how to do an assessment of another person's energy field. We were encouraged to "listen" with our hands and listen for differences in what we felt. Each of us scanned the other. I could feel the excitement in the room as we spoke about what we had noticed when scanning our partner.

"I picked up a prickly sensation around your heart," I mentioned to my partner. Her eyes widened as she said, "I have just been diagnosed with a type of heart condition."

My heart started racing, I knew then that I

would do this form of work at some point in my life, though the training would have to wait until after graduate school.

What did not have to wait was my participation in a Therapeutic Touch practice group, which in turn led me to join a group that offered spiritual support. Sacred Circle included both women from the original introduction to TT and other professional healers. Once again, I believe the universe led me to people that would lend support in my journey through this life. I found total acceptance for who I was and who I was becoming in this group. The pagan practice of Witchcraft that I had developed in New Jersey fit right in. We keep touch via email, yearly retreats and celebrating the Sabbats. The Sabbats are solar, seasonal and represent the cycle of birth, life, death and rebirth. We send requests out for prayers for our loved ones, with miraculous results. We know this connection of light is helping us and the planet we live on.

Soon after graduation from Antioch, with encouragement from my friends in Sacred

Circle, I walked down the hallway of Elliott hospital in Manchester, New Hampshire on a Saturday in October, looking for the room which said 'Therapeutic Touch class here today.' To my relief, I found it. I was filled with curiosity, excitement and more than a little trepidation;" What am I getting myself into?" I wondered.

Therapeutic Touch training began. Our teachers were so welcoming for us newcomers that trepidation soon morphed into a greedy need to know and wonder. The learning of Therapeutic Touch is an ongoing process. I liken it to the refining of a beautiful painting or song that an author can always see ways to improve.

At the time I started my TT training in earnest, I had been working for two years with Helen as my client. I had a good sense of how energy work could help people. The main difference was that while energy work with Helen was spiritually based, Therapeutic Touch was scientifically based. One benefit of TT is how it allows a way for a practitioner to take energy work out to mainstream patients. I felt this would be a good answer to my questions about how to pursue a career in energy medicine. Including Therapeutic Touch in my practice was a great addition to my graduate work and spiritual training. Over the years I spent much of my time teaching TT classes and, at the same time, incorporating TT into my own practice as a Psychotherapist Energy Healer.

TT reinforced the ability to be grounded that I had learned in Bioenergetics. Daily meditation and centering exercises is the cornerstone of my personal healing practice. One of the most engaging ways I learned to meditate was by participating in several meditation workshops at Pumpkin Hollow Farm in New York. These experiences dovetailed into my practice of Therapeutic Touch.

The practitioner prepares by doing a centering exercise. From a calm place, the practitioner approaches the patient with an intention to help or heal. Our intention as practitioners is what makes Therapeutic Touch unique. It is my experience that TT often reaches people in ways that other medical treatments may not. Clinical studies have shown that our energy field as human beings, responds to healing energy.

Witness my sister Martha, who has lived 94 years and has recently been diagnosed with Alzheimer's. She doesn't remember an abundance of things, including some of her family and friends. In the middle of a visit she says to me, "What should we do now?"

"How about you get a rest and some TT?"

"Oh, yes, let's do that." Her face lights up and she smiles.

We help her to bed, she closes her eyes: a peaceful look comes over her face as if previous TT experiences creep into her consciousness. Clearly some part of her has held onto the feelings that come with a Therapeutic Touch treatment. The energy of Therapeutic Touch gets through to her and comes back to her, even as the rest of her memory fails her. This is worth all the years of training and work that allow me to be competent at this modality and bring it to my sister. When the treatment is finished, I quietly leave the room. Martha sleeps peacefully. I believe she was reached by and remembered TT at a time when most other recent memories were no longer available to her.

Through intense training we learn to listen for cues in the palms of our hands. We also gain other cues from all of our sensate faculties. The underlying principle of this modality is that everyone has an energy field. By calling on the universal healing energy, the practitioner helps recipients to do their own healing. Therapeutic Touch is a modern interpretation of several ancient healing practices.

Music plays a large part of my TT practice as well. I sing to clients during treatments. A friend once told someone at a Therapeutic Touch group, "If Dorothea gives you a treatment and you don't get a song, ask for your money back." After taking Intermediate TT training at Pumpkin Hollow Retreat Center, New York and

Advanced training at Camp Indralaya on Orcas Island, Washington, along with several years of additional training in various settings, I became a credentialed practitioner and teacher of Therapeutic Touch. I feel deeply privileged and blessed to have had training at these workshops with Therapeutic Touch's founders: Dora Kunz and Delores Krieger, R.N. PhD. My traditional training as a psychotherapist, working through my Kundalini experience and the healing work I learned with Helen, along with my Therapeutic Touch Training allowed me to begin a practice that included all of these modalities. Teaching TT gave me the ability to reach more people.

Therapeutic Touch taught me to trust that the outcome of any treatment was not in my hands. A major part of what I have taught in TT classes is letting go of the outcome. As a practitioner, I am a conduit for healing energy; the people receiving the treatment facilitate their own healing. TT also encouraged my ability to listen and trust my intuition.

The energy work I learned with Helen

increased my capacity for listening, being truly present, and working with spirits who exist in a dimension other than this earth. TT reinforced my work with Helen.   I became whole, grounded, and competent as a healer. All of this was life altering; describing it here only scratches the surface of how it served me. While I was learning these two different ways of being a healer, my spiritual life was taking on a life of its own. Again, some of my experiences were more easily integrated than others.

CHAPTER TEN

MYSTICAL AND MAGICAL TIMES

In late 1992, two years into my work with Helen and near the beginning of my Therapeutic Touch training, I began having meditations and experiences that would take me to "other worlds," and I experienced the feeling of leaving my body. Around this time, I also began hearing Spiritual messages from other dimensions in words rather than pictures. I believe that having a near death experience in 1971 helped me understand that what was going on was real.

Even so, as I sit down to read my personal journal from 1993, I think – this stuff is nuts, no one will believe this. I don't even believe it, though the writings bring back the memories that confirm its reality. I still think – *this is crazy nonsense – she made it up* – but she is me! I am blown away by the absurdity of it all.

I believe, and my studies have verified for me, that many people experience these or other unusual spiritual events. Perhaps we must do some healing work first so that the experiences do not move us out of spiritual wonder and into psychosis. In the 1970s, the effects of my childhood trauma caused me to succumb to hallucinations and triggered a psychotic break. By the 1990s, after so much of my healing had taken place, I had enough ego strength and professional help to move through these spiritual experiences with wonder. The richness of the unusual experiences also helped to further the process toward wholeness. Given my two very different experiences, I made the decision in graduate school to write my research project on the 'Differences between Psychosis and Spiritual Emergence.'

What follows are dated journal entries from this time period of my life.

March 28, 1993

It is 3:20 am – I wake with one of those, Oh, my god I'm going to be sick for three days headaches. I am sleeping at my sister Martha's house for the night. I heard some noise and thought it was my stomach moaning at first but I think it was tones of the voices. Looked out the window – there was a weird pink light and fog – the head ache was very bad – I asked what to do, and the answer came: "go in your purse and get the Fiorinal that is in there, take two Tylenol, and the one Fiorinal, some flower essences, caffeine tea and elevate your head using at least three pillows. Put a hot face cloth on your face, sit on toilet, wrap blanket around you and let your body evacuate; then go back to bed and try to rest." I did everything that the voices told me to do. The headache got better in thirty minutes, very fast. I sat there watching the strange pink light with tears running down my face. I was so grateful for this relief. I asked "are you from the Pleiades?" They laughed and said "no, but we are from another dimension." I thought I might see a ship. They said, "Not yet – in New Hampshire, soon.

April 5, 1993
During my meditation I looked out my window and saw a reflection of the moon. Then the moon separated into two halves and the two halves went around each other. It came back together again and came toward me, getting a little smaller, almost seeming to sit on the telephone wire at one point. I blinked my eyes to clear this image, but when I opened them, the moon was still on the wire. "Yikes", I thought, "this stuff is too weird". Stay tuned, my spirit seemed to say: there is more to come.

Early in April of 1993, I attended a small gathering of women about twenty-five miles from my home. This group was made up of individuals who were having unusual spiritual experiences; we gathered to support each other. When we went around the circle to introduce ourselves, one of the women said she was from the same town as I. We thought it strange we had not met until in this group.

The group began with a brief meditation; we asked for spiritual beings on the other side of the veil to be with us. My mother came. I saw her as I last remembered her. Our hostess also "felt" her presence. She asked, "Does anyone here have a woman named Vicki, kind of a large woman?" I knew that she also saw my mother. The ability to see spirits who had left this planet was relatively new to me at that time. I said nothing. I needed to process this internally prior to speaking about it, and I wondered why my mother was there.

Before the end of this meeting, Kathryn and I agreed to get together for tea sometime soon at her home. She showed me that day, a couple black and white pictures of drawings she had done. They were drawings that came to her in the night. She did not consider herself an artist, but would wake up in the night and know exactly how to draw these remarkable drawings. They are drawings that seemed to come through her and were not of her, as she described the process. They appeared as something from another time, place, or dimension.

On the Sunday night after the meeting, I felt a vibration and a pulling out of my body. I saw colors – greens, pinks, and lavender – in various shapes. Some were spheres, some more like streaks. I was not asleep; this was not a dream. I thought of it as a type of meditative state.

Two days later I visited Kathryn's house. She took me into the room where most of the drawings were. It was a small, naturally lit room, and the drawings, which were several different sizes, hung on the walls or rested on small tables. They depicted abstract forms and symbols, drawn completely by hand without the use of any art utensils other than the pencils. This was the first time I had seen any of her drawings other than the two black and white pictures that she showed me at our meeting. When I looked at these drawings, I burst into tears. Then I sat in their midst in stunned silence taking in the message they gave. I felt every pain I had ever felt in this whole lifetime, and, at the same time, I felt very light and totally peaceful. Tears ran down my face. One of the drawings had the same shapes and colors that I had seen during the previous Sunday night meditation.

On some spiritual level, I understood that everything is lovable and healable. All pain, grief and turmoil, as well the joy and love we experience, together bring a peace that is impossible to describe adequately. In Ruby Nelson's book "The Door of Everything," she discusses the "peace that passes understanding, the love that conquers all." Having experienced this peace on a physical level, not as an academic idea, changed my life – again.

When our visit was over, I asked Kathryn to visit my house for tea soon. A few weeks passed and she had one reason or another that prevented her from coming. In the meantime, I told a few people about this wonderful woman I had met named Betsy. Each time I said that, I caught myself and exclaimed, "Why do I keep doing that? Her name is Kathryn." I did not understand why this was happening.

One morning during meditation, I asked my guides; I refer to the voices that spoke to me in March at Martha's house, as my guides. "Okay, why do I keep referring to Kathryn as Betsy? It is rude and I'm afraid I will call her that directly." The reply was, "She is the same spirit who was your sister Betsy, who died in the early 1930's."

"What!"

They repeated slowly as if they were speaking to a child: "She... is... the... same... spirit... who... was... your... sister..."

"Okay, okay, I heard you," I replied. Then, to myself, *oh my God – what am I supposed to do with that information? No wonder my mother showed up the day we met.*

In May, Kathryn agreed to come over for tea. When she came to the house she said: "I've had some resistance to coming here, Dorothea, not sure why." I said nothing; she walked in. We drank tea and talked. During our conversation, Kathryn told me she always thought that she had a "lost sister" out there somewhere. That maybe her mother had a baby out of wedlock that no one would talk about. She had had this feeling most of her life. Her parents were both dead now, so she had no one to ask.

After a while, I brought a picture of my mother to show Kathryn. It was of my brother Gordon, me, and my mother in front of the house where we had lived. Kathryn said, "I know this place. I recognize that small wall in the driveway. Where is this?" The house I grew up in had a very narrow cement wall on either side of the driveway. I've never seen one like it anywhere else.

"It's in Abington, Massachusetts."

"I grew up in Abington," she said.

"Well, this is on Lewis Road," I replied.

"I grew up on Lewis Road," she said.

I began to feel a bit agitated. "*Well, this is above South Street.*" Lewis Road had two definite neighborhoods, above South Street and below South Street. I began moving back just a tiny bit from Kathryn.

"I grew up above South Street," she said. "What was your name then?" I felt stunned and answered by rote, telling her my last name.

"I remember walking by that house every day on the way to school and thinking there was some secret in that house," she said but I never saw any people there."

I was incredulous. She never saw any people? How can that be? There were thirteen of us living there.

Meanwhile, I did not say a word to Kathryn about the information that had been given to me by my guides. I was freaked out at the fact that we had grown up four doors away from each other and didn't meet until 50 years later in New Hampshire. By this time, I felt very strange and more than a little nauseous. We talked about how it would be fun to go down to Abington together some day and see the old street. Kathryn left that day without hearing anything about the knowledge I had. I did not know what, if anything, I was to do with the information about our being sisters. Trusting my own intuition and spiritual guidance was very helpful because, clearly, there wasn't anything for me to do with the information at that time.

The next morning my phone rang. Kathryn, saying, "Alright Dorothea, how much of this did you already know?" Smiling, I ask her if she wants to go out for coffee. Kathryn agreed, and I picked her up. Off we went to the local bagel shop.

In the car on our way to the bagel shop, I asked, "Kathryn, has anyone ever called you Betsy? Or would the name Betsy seem strange to you should I call you that?" Kathryn replied, "No, it doesn't actually, and you are not the first person to call me that. Why? Then, in a 'what's this all about' kind of voice, she asked, "*Why do you want to know?*" I could hear in her voice that she knew there was more.

I told her the story and the information given to me by my guides. Her face lit up and she said "I know its true – I'm the lost sister!" I said "You have no idea. Let's go get that bagel. You have lots of sisters!"

I filled her in on how many children were in our family and a bit of our history, such as when Mom died, where most our siblings were living and who was close by that might want to meet her. Over time, I introduced her to four of our sisters. They were delighted to meet her. Janet told stories of when Kathryn had been baby Betsy. My sisters wholeheartedly embraced Kathryn as their sister which made for an easy gathering. Sometimes I called her KB.

During the following year, we had many good times together. We did go down to see Lewis Road. The day we visited, the people who lived in my old home were in the process of chopping up and clearing out the cement wall in the driveway. We asked for a piece of it and were happy to receive one each. It felt serendipitous. We also went to the cemetery where both Kathryn's parents and my parents, along with Betsy are buried. When we got there, I took her to the grave-site of my parents. She pointed to another grave-site very close by, where her parents were buried. We both agreed this was another of a long line of coincidences, seeing as how Abington Cemetery covers a lot of ground.

At the beginning of 1994, I moved to North Carolina, but Kathryn and I stayed in touch. Once she sent me one of her drawings. In the note that came with it, she said, "The 'guys' insisted that I send this to you." (Kathryn referred to her drawings collectively as "the guys.") I am thrilled to have that drawing.

Until recently, it had been several years since we have seen each other. Kathryn is like so many others of my friends in that it didn't matter how long we go without seeing each other, we are able to pickup right where we left off upon meeting again. We speak briefly on the phone occasionally so I know she is still out there. I believe that this woman came into my life so that I would understand that the past life experiences I have witnessed throughout this journey are real and that I've been here on this planet many times. I also believe that we were brought together to support each other in our spiritual journeys. We two shared an adventurous time together. We laughed a lot and wondered who would ever believe us. It was an enriching time of my life that helped me to go on and trust this crazy journey.

During this time, other unusual experiences continued to come into my life, and I continued to document them for myself.

April 27, 1993

There were seven crystal–like beings, sort of in a cluster standing around my bed, but not attached. They were light and shiny and, not very long. They spoke to me, but I couldn't understand at first. I asked if they were channeled beings (the question seemed to come to me). They said yes, we came to tell you things you need to know. They sort of spread out a little – they didn't stay long - they had things to tell me that I would use and tell others.

Later that same day, at Helen's, I raised Kundalini again. I felt it go all the way up through my head. The Crystal Beings were there for a few minutes just before the energy moved.

I had the sense I wanted to say to them "Okay, Okay, I got it! Need to lighten up!"

May 4, 1993

During my birthday meditation, I saw myself as a Monk, possibly Tibetan, in a large chamber meditating. Great light and energy came through me. I heard high pitch and low pitch sounds felt vibrations and saw energy come out of my hands, healing the earth long time ago. It felt like I was being shown another lifetime so I would know I could do this kind of work again

During meditation at a workshop I attended, and then several times after, I saw a small red crystal. It was situated at the base of my spine. I asked some friends who knew much more than I did about crystals if they knew what kind of crystal it might be. Most had not heard of a red stone that also came as a crystal. One night in meditation my mind went to a place where there was a red crystal cave. There were other beings there above the cave and I was directed into the cave. The cave seemed to be the source of the red crystal I had seen previously during meditations. I felt the energy of the crystal cave permeating me. The other beings seemed concerned. When I came back in my body, I had a headache.

In the fall of that year I went to a Rock and Mineral Show that is held yearly in New Hampshire. I thought I was only going to accompany a friend, but as we got closer, my head began to feel quite light. It was a large gathering with many vendors. One of the first I stopped at had a red crystal, the size and color of the one from my meditations. My friend Isabelle was there and she said, "I think you are supposed to buy that, Dorothea."

I moved on through the gathering, almost in an altered state of consciousness, not yet knowing what to do. At another place I saw small straight crystals that reminded me of my crystal friends. At that moment, my seven crystal friends showed up. "Get one for each of us!" I heard. *I quickly looked around to see if anyone saw me talking to myself or saw anything strange about me.* About the same time another friend showed up and I told her what had happened. "Buy them," she said, "it's not like they are telling you to spend tons of money! They only cost a dollar each! Buy them!" It was a miracle to me that she did not even question that crystal beings came and told me that. I bought the crystals.

Later, on my way out, I stopped by the counter that had the red crystal. I knew I was to get this. The man who was selling it said, "Oh, thank God you came back. I put the crystal under the counter because I knew you were to have it and I was afraid someone else would buy it before you came back. Isabelle knew also, so she and I have already decided how I should wrap it for you so you can wear it as a necklace!"

I once again felt blown away by how this all happened. I have the crystal and wear it whenever I am working with a client. The physical manifestation of that crystal helped me to understand and know that information I was receiving from the world of spirit was very real and was to guide my life going forward.

April 30, 1993
Helen loaned me my first healing table and some friends brought it up to my apartment. We set it down in living room and I felt a shot of energy go through it.

May 6, 1993
During a meditation, I began to feel the "tightness" of my apartment. I felt like I needed a bigger space, for the table and for me. I felt I was expanding and needed more space.

May 21, 1993
During this meditation, I saw a bright cone of light going through me. I felt my head expanding and pain in my head for which I took pain medication. My body seemed to be moving in circle. My head actually did get somewhat larger during this time as I could no longer wear hats that used to fit me.

In October of 1993, due to a friend's

recommendation, I participated in a Sacred Fire Walk. A local Native American woman led the walk. Fire Walks are sacred rituals in which individuals walk with bare feet across very hot coals if, and only if, they are guided forth by inner knowing. The Fire Walk stirred many emotions for me. It is my custom to have a prayer request for the Universe when participating in Sacred Ritual. My prayer for this ritual was that I would be shown a proper place to do my healing work. Even though I was skeptical about the walk, it seemed right to be there and to support the other participants.

All the material that went into the fire was blessed by our leader before the fire was lit. The fire was very large; we circled it for several hours, calling out our prayers. The leader spoke about not walking across unless we were sure Spirit intended us to. She encouraged us to call out our fears- *I'm afraid I will get burned, afraid I will do it by mistake, this whole thing is stupid anyway-* on and on until the flames had burned down. The helpers took long rakes and raked the coals, leaving only one layer. She spoke of how hot the coals were (1200 to 1500 degrees) and how each individual would know if it was right to do this.

"If you are not sure, do not walk. People can get burned," she explained. "This is not a mystical experience. It is about paying close attention to your inner guidance and trusting what you hear, knowing with a certainty what you should do. Some of you are not meant to do this right now, tonight."

Everyone took off their shoes and socks and kept circling the fire whether or not they were going to step on the coals, out of respect for those who did walk that night. My feet got very cold. The woman next to me told me she had done this once and was there that night to support others who would walk. At one point, I joked to her, "My feet will get so cold, and I'll walk across just to get some relief." She replied, "You will know if you are supposed to walk."

Near the end of the night, I saw a friend on the opposite side of the circle. There was a space right next to her. I knew that space was for me. I did not make a decision to step on the coals; I only knew that my heart or something inside me was pulling me into that space. I got there by going across the coals.

When I got to the other side, my feet were even colder. They felt as if they might fall off. I thought, at first, they were burned because the cold was so severe it hurt, but there was no burning or damage to my feet that night. All was well, despite what my, or anyone's rational mind knew would happen.

My head felt so strange when it was time to leave. "Could I please follow you home?" I asked a friend, "I have no idea where I am or how to get home." The Fire Walk had put me in an altered state of consciousness and spirit helped get me home safely. On the way home, my friend pointed to my exit off the highway. It was another 20-minute ride for me from the turnoff. I don't remember the rest of the ride home. Like Aladdin's magic carpet, my car seemed to travel under its own steam.

This ritual changed how I live my life. After that night I was able to follow my heart, spirit, guides, messages that came in unusual forms, and other ways of knowing.

The fire walk and its aftermath of trusting showed me how to move forward with what I knew to be the right thing for me to do.

CHAPTER ELEVEN

SPIRITUAL QUEST

In the fall of 1993, I received three fliers in the mail for a workshop entitled "*The Difference between Psychosis and Spiritual Emergence.*" I felt that any time something came to me in threes, it was a spiritual message and I would do well to pay attention. I was not aware of being on any list for these workshops. Certainly, I knew I was not on any list three times. I was surprised to get a flier for a workshop with this title at all because that was the title of my graduate school oral presentation two years before and I had done myriad amounts of research on the subject. I picked up the brochure, read it and had a strong feeling it would be best for me to go.

The weekend workshop was at a mental health center in Asheville, North Carolina that did not have any facilities for rooming. Before going, I told my sisters about the conference. Then I asked them, "Alright, we must have upwards of a million relatives; do any of you know of one near Asheville, North Carolina? Someone I might stay with while I am attending this conference?"

"Well," one of my sisters replied; "I used to live in a convent down there. I could call them and see if they could offer you hospitality." She called and they agreed. Turns out the conference was a five-minute walk from the convent; coincidence; perhaps, but surely, serendipitous.

I remember sitting at the conference, and, although I enjoyed the speakers and small group sessions, I kept wondering. What am I doing here? *This is not new information for me.* I wondered what the real reason for my being there could be.

I enjoyed staying at the convent. One of the

sisters remembered my family and in particular asked about a five- year-old child who used to come and play in a convent they have served in Abington, Massachusetts. Smiling, I let them know that I was the five-year-old they remembered. Talking with three of the sisters who had remembered me as a child felt a bit like being in a time machine. My memories of being in their convent came back to me. It was called St. Genevieve Academy and was on Lewis Street in Abington, a few doors away from my childhood home.

In one of my conversations with the sisters, I remember thinking. *It is remarkable that the same sisters who offered me hospitality as a child are extending hospitality to me now, 50 years later.* I said to Sister Joan; "I have a sense that God is going to ask me to move here to Asheville. One of the sisters said, "We would love to have you living near us." I was also beginning to feel nervous about that possibility. When leaving for home, I agreed to keep the sisters informed of my plans.

After I got home, I did a lot of praying and meditating, asking for guidance. At one point, I asked my spirit guides if that, indeed, I was being asked to move to Asheville. The excitement in my body told me that spirit was giving me a resounding yes in answer to my question.

I also asked, "Would my going down a few times to look for a job and perhaps a place to live be best?" The answer came back. "No, pack up your belongings, store them here for now and get in your car and go." There was now no doubt in my mind that spirit was asking me to take this leap of faith, trust my guidance and go.

While still in New Hampshire, I applied for a full-time teaching position at the college where I was teaching psychology. The position was only for one year, and I thought, this would be perfect to give me a year to feel my way towards moving. It was not to be. I was not offered the position at the college. I was to go, and soon.

A few friends did not exactly support this decision to go. "You can't just pick up and move without a job or a place to stay! How will you survive? How will you earn your living?" Isn't that an interesting concept, I thought, that one has to earn a living, not just live! My sense was that the underlying question was really: "Why are you leaving us!?" Most of my sisters and close friends valiantly gave me their support, though I suspect some thought my madness might be back!

One day I got a message, while meditating, to call my friend, Robin.

"Hi Robin," I said. "I got a message to call you today. I don't know why."

"I think I know," she said. "We have a ghost in our house. We are not afraid, but we were hoping you would come over and see if you can find out what he wants."

I agreed to go the following Monday. Robin knew that I had training as a medium and was sometimes in touch with beings on "the other side of the veil" as we say in pagan circles.

In my Sunday meditation, my message to go to North Carolina very soon was quite clear. On Monday at Robin's, I was able to contact the spirit in her house. I was able to help her understand why he was there and what he needed from her and her husband. As we were talking afterward, I told of my going to North Carolina, more or less as soon as possible. Robin said, "We have a large empty barn where you can store your furniture and an empty room inside for things like your mattress and couch." I just sat there, a bit stunned. Here is my storage unit!

I felt a bit of shock about the ways in which the universe provides, and instinctively I knew I had to go. In the end, the universe did provide me with everything I needed when I arrived there.

It is January, 1994, and I am alone in my car driving to Asheville, North Carolina on a spiritual quest. At least, that is how it feels to me because I am moving there without a job and without really understanding why I am going. With me are the personal belongings that will help me to survive until I find a place to live and can send for my furniture.

It will take two to three days to get there as I am only driving in daylight hours and making frequent stops to stretch. Sometimes I have the radio on or a CD of music that I love. It is warm and comfortable inside my car. This belies the fact that I am not feeling comfortable at all about this trip. Sometimes I am literally screaming about how scared I am. Anger and fear have me yelling at the Divine: "I know you want to me to do this and I am doing it, but I'm not happy about it and I'm very frightened!" Why does this have to be? I so wish that I were not doing this alone. I wish that I had a traveling companion or a life partner to help with this journey. But then it wouldn't really be a spiritual quest now, would it, Dorothea?

At the time I traveled, I believed I should have been able to do this with less fear. After that experience, I understand that I just need to move through whatever fear is there. I am always taken care of by the universe and trust that wherever I am led is where I am supposed to be. How things worked out in North Carolina is not nearly as important as knowing that going on faith is what is important. I knew that a space would be there for me. And it was.

I found an apartment that was perfect for me, and the landlady and I became close friends. In line with my work, I became a North Carolina Licensed Professional Counselor to include using TT in my practice, a credentialed Therapeutic Touch teacher and taught psychology courses in two local community colleges. I first taught TT in the mental health center which held the workshop on Psychosis vs. Spiritual Emergence, and continued to teach TT in several other establishments, including a Catholic retreat center. I became a member of an Asheville group of alternative healers. So many venues opened up to teach and practice energy healing that I got a sense that the people in that area were hungry for something to complement, medically, what they had always done. I never doubted the move was right for me.

In 1989, prior to leaving New Jersey, I had

had a card reading from a psychic woman who had been doing this kind of work her whole life. She said I would be moving up north to New Hampshire and I would stay there five years and then move to either North or South Carolina or Virginia. At the time of this reading, all I could say was, "I can't imagine moving to one of those places." She stated, as fact, "It doesn't matter - you're going."

CHAPTER TWELVE

AND THE BEAT GOES ON...

As I write this, I feel grounded, at peace, and very happy to be doing something perfectly normal for me: writing and telling my story. I recognize that this grounded, peaceful way of being could never have happened without all the years I spent healing and being spiritually awake. Life for me is about catching the joy of living nearly all the time. I truly love the woman I have become. And so, it is.

I have never doubted that moving to North Carolina was right for me; it has only been in the process of writing this book that I understand why. I was sent there to experience what would bring me closer to Divine Love. All my experiences before and while living there helped me to realize that the purpose of my life is to be at One with the Divine within and to Love.

While I lived down south, I became grounded in the understanding that it really doesn't matter what we call ourselves and that we are all part of the same spiritual energy. I am a practicing Witch and call this energy the vibration of Divine Love or Spirit. This knowing is the 'take-away' from my time in the South. While there, I honed the spiritual listening skills I had learned. My intuitive mind, Spirit, directs my life.

During my time in North Carolina, there were many communities and churches that called to me. One Sunday, it came to me to go to the local Catholic Church in Swannanoa to sing. I had met the Pastor briefly at the convent in Asheville and he invited me to come and sing sometime. I went up to the organist, told her why I had come, and her face lit up. "Can you sing the Ave Maria?" she asked. "Yes, but I can't tell you what key I sing it in." "Just start singing;

I will follow you on the organ." I felt an uplifting energy doing this. It was very similar to many other experiences I had with other spiritual groups:

- Being welcomed into the of Baha'i community
- Singing in multicultural choir
- Playing guitar music for New Age religious group
- Being part of the Unity Church in Asheville
- Speaking at a Sunday service for the Spiritualist church
- Singing at a Baptist Revival and,
- My Ordination as a Pastor in the Church of the Sacred Earth.

The circle is complete. I'm home and the essence of my being in the world is joyful, painful and pretty well balanced. In a family as large as ours, there are many joys and many sorrows. I still cry fully, not holding back, and I still laugh really hard and often. I credit my mother with making laughter a big part of my adult life – always. I've known for a very long time that tears and laughter balance each other out. These days I am grateful for both. The difference from years ago is extraordinary. Tears in the past were wrenching and difficult; tears now are wrenching and difficult. The missing component is depression. Grief (which sometimes seems unbearable), sadness, and long bouts of crying do not mean depression. That illness is gone. Blessed Be.

How the illness left can be observed in the following dream that came twice on the same night, very late in my healing process with Helen.

Life is a balancing act - a lot of layers that I have to balance. Each has a ball and then a square piece of glass on top. I have to get the glass on the ball just right before the next layer can go on. These are on top of a large hill or small mountain that had a hole at the top for the first layer. There were people around saying it was my job to go up there and balance it. I felt like they were waiting for me to do this. There were a lot of other people that I had to help along the way. At each step up the mountain there was someone who needed something from me.

The dream says to me, in Jungian terms, that each person who needed something from me as I went up the mountain was me, at different stages of my recovery. Each step I took made the next possible:

- The support from my family and friends early on made it possible for me to acknowledge my illness and begin healing in the psychiatric hospital.
- The strength I gained from my hospital stays, and all the decisions following, brought me to Bioenergetics and making the mind/body connection in my work with Eli Rubin.
- The work with Eli enabled me to do the energy work with Helen and feel safe

enough being touched.

- Without the work with Helen, I could not have done the fire walk, listening and trusting to move into the space across the fire.
- Finishing the Fire walk gave me the courage to go to North Carolina.
- And without my experiences in North Carolina, I would not be living my current balanced life.

I recently received one seemingly mundane message: "You have been looking for two yellow throw pillows to decorate your new home. Go to Marshall's now, you will find the pillows there." It was 7:15 pm. I never went out shopping at night, but I took the advice. They were there as promised and now complement my living room. How did I know this? Was it my inner self, my Spirit, my guides from other dimensions? Faith and trust come in many forms.

Music continues to be a part of my spiritual practice. Each summer I spend a week at a wondrous music camp and I also am part of an on-going song writing circle. The first year at summer music camp, I took a song writing class that opened up a whole new world for me. Turns out, I can write songs. The first two songs I wrote are in memory of the singing my family did growing up.

Writing music is very healing for me; it makes me laugh and cry. It makes me cry a good deal, which means it moves the sadness out of my being. Writing a song for my sister Eileen after her unexpected passing helped me to move on from that pain. The day after she died, I woke up crying and continued to cry most of the day. The pain seemed unbearable. My daughter Emma called in the early afternoon and asked, "Mom, how are you?"

"Well, other than I cannot stop crying and I can barely move off my bed, you mean, other than that, how am I?" We both laughed, got through the funeral and I began to write her song.

And the beat goes on!

I sing everywhere I go. My voice rings out every time I visit my current favorite grocery store. I receive lots of positive feedback from people who are shopping at the same time I am. One year around the December holidays, I was singing an old time Christmas Carol. A man near me stopped his wife and said as he pointed to me: "Listen, she is right! We should slow down and enjoy the holidays. Let's have fun shopping...listen to her!" I thanked him and he said, "No, we thank you for the reminder." It was a happy moment in time; several people around us were also smiling at the exchange.

And just last year, I wrote a song that says it all, "This book I write is my song."

Transforming a very difficult, abusive childhood into my current love of life is exceptional. Never mind that it took 50 years. That it happened at all is further evidence to me that angels and the Divine were with me every step of the way. I know that the Divine is in everyone and everything, including my dad. I am grateful for my entire journey, all of it. No exceptions.

© June 2017 – Dorothea Juno-Johnston

AFTERWARD

This book was originally copy righted and completed in June of 2017, sure this book was finished, complete so we thought in 2017 and now it's finally getting published in 2023. What were you waiting for, you might ask? Divine timing.

Even though we know everything changes in life, in the last several years the whole world has shifted as if we are all now in another dimension. Certainly I have changed in so many ways.

What has stayed the same for me during the publishing of this book, and perhaps, the writing of it, is my excitement in knowing that the Universe is Love, Energy and Light. We are One, we are the Divine one. Learning to listen to that one within me...... got me here.

Take what you will, leave what you must. I send wishes for something in these pages to have spoken to you.

Blessed Be

ACKNOWLEDGMENTS

I am most grateful for the myriad of men and women over the years who were with me through the storms, laughter and amazing joy that is life.

Agnes Bray, my favorite teacher, helped me manage to get through high school intact. Thank you, dear Agnes for seeing in me what I could not say.

Sister Alice Schoettelkotte C.PP.S. for her unfailing support for the last fifty years up to and including reading the first draft of this manuscript.

Nicolia Mehrling, my editor for all the early and late drafts of this manuscript. Above and beyond is how I witness her diligence, skill, and sense of wonder through it all.

I am indebted to the readers of the full manuscript and their feedback: Peg Espinola, Sandra Waddock, Cynthia Abbott, Donna Neubauer, Chris Boehmer, Maureen Egan, Dru Nichols and Ives Grant.

My dear friend, Martha Cochran line edited the entire manuscript. Her friendship, feedback and suggestions were invaluable.

To Bethany Van Wagenen, for her complete confidence in our ability to bring this story out for those who would benefit. A very special thanks to Sandra Waddock for sharing all the research she had done on self-publishing that helped us find the way.

Grateful for Pauline Silveri, R.N., Lorry Roy, R.N. and Elaine Wilk, R.N., my original Therapeutic Touch teachers. We have continued to support each other since we first met in 1990.

I am grateful to Dora Kunz and Delores Krieger, R.N. Ph.D. for being the courageous and brilliant originators of Therapeutic Touch. It was an honor to have been taught TT by these women. To Dora for turning me on to meditation before I ever learned TT.

To Alexander Lowen for his dedication to the creation of Bioenergetics. and spreading the good news of this work through his books and teaching.

For More information Contact: Laurie Ure, a Licensed Independent Clinical Social worker and Certified Bioenergetic Therapist. https://laurieure.com/

APPENDIX

SONGS

Thanksgiving

Dorothea © September 2007

```
G                              D              C     Am        D
At the dining room table lots of young faces, hoping not to be seen

G                       D              C     Am        G
Bless us oh Lord and these Thy gifts, graces, we are bout to receive

G                            D              C              Am        D
Dad cares the turkey at the head of the table; children must be seen and not heard.

G                       D              C              Am        G
Mom serves her mince pie as soon as she's able, dark and light meat from the bird.
```

<u>CHORUS:</u>

```
Em          Am      D              C          Am              D
Open the windows for I cannot hear, came a deep friendly voice from next door.

     C          Am      D        G         C              (D)  G
We'd gathered together to do the Lord's dishes, and we sang louder than before.
```

```
G                            D              C              Am        D
In a house full of turmoil where love seemed to hide, steady Stan Forman we adored.

G                       D              C              Am              G
He helped us go places of safety inside, and sometimes we danced cross the floor
```

<u>CHORUS</u>

```
G                            D              C              Am        D
Yes, we had a neighbor who just did his thing, not many long-words he'd say.

G                       D              C     Am        G
Just how are you doing? And let me hear you sing, saving our souls I daresay
```

<u>CHORUS</u>:

171

SURVIVAL

Dm
Music helped us all get by

I remember singing in the kitchen
    I remember Singing in the kitchen – underlines are repeat lines
–like an echo

Each new song we heard we tried

I remember singing in the kitchen
    I remember Singing in the kitchen

Harmonies ringing out (this line in harmony)

**We were in tune with each other – (this line we sing all together –
the melody)**

No one missed a beat….
    No one

I remember singing in the kitchen
    Singing in the kitchen – repeat 3 times together.

Dorothea © 2007

Poem put to music late 2008

Updated June 2009

CHOICES   Capo 1st fret

CHORUS:
```
Am                    E7              E                        Am
Each day I work on my book      A song comes into my head
Dm                    Am          E        E7        E
Not a song,    it's a doorway        to a chapter instead
```


```
Am                              E7              Am
Seems I have a choice to make  Comes up every day
Dm                    Am          E                E7
Write a song or my memoir    the choice is here to stay
```


```
Am                      E7                      Am
Treat each chapter as a song   work on it each day.
Dm                      Am        E                E7
Begin and end with the chorus, verses are what I have to say
```

CHORUS:


```
Am                                  E7                  Am
First write what you're going to say, work on it each day.
Dm                          Am      E      E7
Then write details of the chapter, perfect lines come my way.
```

```
Am                  E7                      Am
New songs they fill my heart, come up every day
Dm                      Am          E                    Am
These words I write are my song.    Put in my book as I may
```

CHORUS:

© Dorothea –April 2015

Choices

Transcription by: Sister Alice Schottlekotte

NOTES & SUGGESTED READINGS

Chapter One: In the Beginning

References:

1. Jensen, Derrick. *A Language Older Than Words,*
   pgs.3,4

Suggested Reading:

1. Jensen, Derrick. *A Language Older Than Words.*
   VT: Chelsea Green Publishing Co., 2004.

Chapter Four: It's Ringing in the Kitchen, or; Who's Really Nuts here Anyway

References:

1. Styron, William. *Darkness Visible: A Memoir of
   Madness,* pg. 68

Suggested Readings:

1. Cutting, Linda Katherine. *Memory Slips: A Memoir of
   Music and Healing.* New York: HarperCollins,1997.

2. Styron, William. *Darkness Visible: A Memoir of
   Madness.* New York: Random House, 1990.

Chapter Six: Death with Dignity

Suggested Readings:

1. Fanslow-Brunjes, Cathleen, M.A., R.N. *The Four Stages of Hope: Using the Power of Hope to Cope with Dying.* Sanger, CA: Quill Driver Books, 2008.

2. Fitzpatrick, Jeanne, M.D. & Eileen M. , J.D.. *A Better Way of Dying: How to Make the Best Choices at the End of Life.* Toronto, ON: Penguin Books, 2010.

Chapter Seven: Moving from Surviving to Thriving

References:

1. **www.bioenergetic-therapy.com**
2. Starhawk, *Dreaming the Dark*, © by: Miriam Simos
3. Adler, Margot, *Drawing Down the Moon*, pg. 99

Suggested Readings - BIOENERGETICS:

1. Lowen, A. Bioenergetics: The revolutionary therapy that uses the language of the body to heal problems of the mind. NY: Penguin Arkana, 1975.

2. Lowen, A. Joy: The surrender to the body and to life. NY: Penguin Arkana, 1995.

Suggested Readings - WITCHCRAFT/PAGAN:

3. Adler, Margot. *Drawing Down The Moon.* Boston: Beacon Press, 1979.

4. Starhawk. *Dreaming The Dark*, © by Miriam Simos. Boston: Beacon Press, 1982.

5. Starhawk. *The Spiral Dance*. New York: Harper & Row, 1979.

Chapter Nine: Therapeutic Touch (TT)

Notes:

- The following definition is taken from **http://therapeutic-touch.org/**
Therapeutic Touch is a holistic, evidence-based therapy that incorporates the intentional and compassionate use of universal energy to promote balance and well-being.

Suggested Readings:

1. Krieger, Dolores, Ph.D. R.N. *Accept.ing Your Power to Heal: The Personal Practice of Therapeutic Touch*. Santa Fe, NM: Bear & Company Publishing, 1993.

2. Krieger, Dolores, Ph.D. R.N. *Therapeutic Touch Inner Workbook*. Santa Fe, NM: Bear & Company, 1997

3. Kunz, Dora with Krieger, Dolores, Ph.D., R.N. *The Spiritual Dimension of Therapeutic Touch*. VT: Bear and Company, 2004.

4. Macrae, Janet. *Therapeutic Touch: A Practical Guide*. NY: Alfred A. Knopf, 1988.

Chapter Ten: Mystical and Magical Times

Suggested Works:

1. Nicholas Roerich Museum. www.roerich.org (Russian Artist) *(Some of his work reminds one of Kathryn's drawings)*

Suggested Readings:

1. Kandinsky, Wassilly. *Concerning The Spiritual in Art.* Courier Corporation, 2012.

2. Nelson, Ruby. *The Door of Everything.* CA: DeVorss & Company Publisher, 1963.

Chapter Eleven: Spiritual Awakening

References:

1. Sannella, Lee. *Kundalini: Classical and Clinical*, pgs. 101-102

Suggested Readings:

1. Dass, Ram. *Miracle of Love: Stories about Neem Karoli Baba.* NY: E.P. Dutton, 1979.

2. Grof, Stanislav, M.D. And Christina, Eds. *Spiritual Emergency: When Personal Transformation Becomes a Crisis.* Los Angeles: Jeremy PP. Tarcher, Inc., 1989.

3. Sannella, Lee, M.D. *Kundalini: Psychosis or Transcendence?*, SF: H.S. Dakin Company, 1976.

179

ABOUT THE AUTHOR

Dorothea Juno-Johnston, M.A.

Dorothea is an Internationally known teacher of Psychology, Therapeutic Touch and Music therapy classes. She has taught at Harvard Medical School, Massachusetts General Hospital Psychiatric Department, Findhorn Foundation, Scotland, Living Waters Catholic Reflections Center, North Carolina, Mountain Area Health Education Center, North Carolina, Springfield College, Manchester, New Hampshire. She is also an ordained Minister/Pastor of The Church of the Sacred Earth.

Dorothea's short stories have been published in The Christian Century Bi-Monthly Publication, 2016; Therapeutic Touch International Association, 2015; and The Story of a Music Community: The Unofficial History of SAMW, 2015.

www.junojohnston.com
mysong.gratitude@gmail.com